OLD TESTAMENT WARRIORS

OLD TESTAMENT WARRIORS

The Clash of Cultures in the Ancient Near East

SIMON ELLIOTT

CASEMATE

Oxford & Philadelphia

Published in Great Britain and the United States of America in 2021 by
CASEMATE PUBLISHERS
The Old Music Hall, 106–108 Cowley Road, Oxford OX4 1JE, UK
and
1950 Lawrence Road, Havertown, PA 19083, USA

Hardcover Edition: ISBN 978-1-61200-954-4
Digital Edition: ISBN 978-1-61200-955-1

A CIP record for this book is available from the British Library

Printed and bound in the United Kingdom by TJ Books

Typeset by Versatile PreMedia Services (P) Ltd.

For a complete list of Casemate titles, please contact:

CASEMATE PUBLISHERS (UK)
Telephone (01865) 241249
Email: casemate-uk@casematepublishers.co.uk
www.casematepublishers.co.uk

CASEMATE PUBLISHERS (US)
Telephone (610) 853-9131
Fax (610) 853-9146
Email: casemate@casematepublishers.com
www.casematepublishers.com

Front cover: An early Persian soldier with a bow and spear on a ceramic panel from a
patterned wall in ancient Babylon. Artefact from Iraq saved by the Pergamon
Museum in Berlin. (Shutterstock)

Contents

Introduction

The bold ambition of this book is to detail conflict from the beginning of warfare itself in the Near East and Middle East from around 9,000 BC through to the onset of the Classical period around 500 BC. It encompasses a vast geographic region including the eastern Mediterranean, Levant, Mesopotamia and modern Iran. These are the lands that feature predominantly in the Bible and many other contemporary references.

In terms of scope, the chronology and geography covered are extensive. Therefore, the focus will be on those civilisations that are not only best known to us today, but which also have the most complete datasets to support the narrative. Consequently, the book is broken down into an introduction, a timeline, six chapters and a short conclusion. The timeline is particularly important to allow the reader to follow developments as the book unfolds. The chapters are then broadly chronological, following specific cultures when they were at the height of their power. The first chapter covers the origins of warfare (where the term is defined), and then focuses on the first civilisations of Mesopotamia, these including Sumer, Akkad and the Third Dynasty of Ur. The second chapter looks at the early history of Egypt, Nubia, Canaan and Libya. The third chapter details the origins of chariot warfare, with the Hyksos, Hurrians and Mitanni civilisations. The fourth chapter then turns to Europe with the Minoans, Mycenaeans and Sea Peoples. The fifth chapter returns to the Levant and the Hebrew kingdoms, while the sixth and final chapter looks at the mighty empires of the Hittites, Assyria and Babylon. Specifically, with regards to Egypt, the main period covered here refers to its early history, which is vital to understanding much of what is referenced in the book. This is due to the fact that many works on Egypt tend to concentrate on later ancient Egyptian history, and also because a sister Casemate title specifically focuses on the ancient Egyptian military through its later phases of existence. However, note that the late Egyptian military is still detailed here, though in brief, and later Egyptian-specific events, such as the battle of Kadesh in 1,274 BC are covered elsewhere in the book.

Within each chapter, specific sections detail each culture being referenced. The flow of the book first covers the chronology of the civilisation, then its general background, and finally its military establishment and organisation.

The data used in this work is based on the written word (ancient and primary sources, epigraphy, early accounting practices and graffiti), archaeology, analogy and (where appropriate) anecdote. For the former, we are blessed with multiple sources from many of the cultures mentioned. This includes, of course, the Bible itself, but also many other contemporary references. These include Egyptian hieroglyphics on wall friezes and papyrus scrolls, cuneiform writing tablets from across the entirety of the Levant and Mesopotamia, and the detailed, and often very graphic, wall reliefs of the palaces of the rulers of Assyria, Babylon and the Hittite Empire.

In terms of the definitions used for key words and titles in the book, some explanation is needed here. Firstly, the title of the book references the Old Testament. This is descriptive rather than literal, given the enormous chronological and geographical scope outlined above. Levant is used to describe the territories of modern Cyprus, Turkey, Egypt, Israel, the Palestinian territories, western Jordan and western Syria. Mesopotamia references the territories of modern eastern Jordan and Syria, Iraq and western Iran. To avoid confusion, the term Fertile Crescent has been rarely used, but when it is, it refers to the region tracking the Lower River Nile, Levantine

Mediterranean coast and the Tigris and Euphrates rivers through to the Persian Gulf. Natufian is the name given to the late Mesolithic (Middle Stone Age) culture in the Levant from around 9,000 BC, where sedentary hunter-gatherers started to supplement their diet with wild and, later, cultivated grain. The Neolithic Period (New Stone Age) followed, when farming allowed the sedentary Natufian settlements to coalesce into the first farming communities. The first towns and later cities followed, these being juxtapositional terms in this book, given the differing ways the source material describes such large settlements. Finally, civilisation can be a controversial term depending on one's viewpoint. Here it means complex societies featuring urban settlement, symbolic ways of communicating, a separation from the natural environment and – often in the context of those featured here – social stratification imposed by societal elites.

Timeline

9,000 BC	Jericho founded.
8,250 BC	Pre Pottery Neolithic A (PPNA) walls of Jericho built.
7,000 BC	Pottery made in the region for the first time.
6,800 BC	Farming settlements begin to spread south into Mesopotamia.
6,500 BC	Hassuna culture in northern Mesopotamia first to make painted pottery in the region.
6,000 BC	Samarran culture flourishes in Mesopotamia. Beginning of the Predynastic Egyptian period.
5,900 BC	Ubaid culture flourishes in southern Mesopotamia.
5,500 BC	Farming settlements now found across the entirety of Mesopotamia.
5,400 BC	Ubaid culture replaces Halafian culture in northern Mesopotamia.
4,300 BC	Beginning of the Uruk period of Sumerian expansion.
3,500 BC	Sodom and Gomorrah founded.
3,300 BC	First major towns appear in the Nile Valley.
3,150 BC	Beginning of the Early Dynastic Egyptian period.
3,000 BC	King Narmer of Upper Egypt conquers Lower Egypt, uniting the two for the first time.
2,900 BC	Beginning of the Sumerian Early Dynastic Period.
2,800 BC	End of Nubian A-Group culture.
2,700 BC	Minoan culture begins to flourish in Greece.
2,600 BC	Assyrian city of Assur founded.

2,500 BC	Beginning of Nubian C-Group culture.
2,686 BC	Beginning of the Old Kingdom Egyptian period.
2,668 BC	Accession of Egyptian king Djoser, builder of Egypt's first step pyramid.
2,600 BC	Battle of Uruk.
2,550 BC	Construction begins of the great pyramid of the Egyptian king Khufu.
2,500 BC	King Mesannepadda of Ur conquers Ur and Kish.
2,334 BC	Accession of Sargon the Great in Kish, beginning of period of Akkadian dominance, end of the Sumerian Early Dynastic Period.
2,279 BC	Death of Sargon the Great.
2,254 BC	Accession of Naram-Sin, Akkadian power at its height.
2,250 BC	Sumerian Great Revolt.
2,218 BC	Death of Naram-Sin.
2,193 BC	Collapse of Akkadian Empire.
2,112 BC	Beginning of the Third Dynasty of Ur.
2,100 BC	First evidence of chariots found in *kurgan*, a type of burial mound, found in the Sintashta-Petrovka region at the southern end of the Ural Mountains.
2,004 BC	End of the Third Dynasty of Ur.
2,000 BC	First cities emerge in Crete.
1,975 BC	Beginning of the Middle Kingdom Egyptian period.
1,900 BC	Aamu nomads begin to settle in Nile Delta.
1,813 BC	Accession of Shamshi-Adad I of Assyria.
1,800 BC	Canaanites begin to settle in the Nile Delta, including Hebrew tribes.
1,792 BC	Accession of king Hammurabi in the First Dynastic period in Babylon.
1,752 BC	The Hurrians migrate into northern Syria.
1,700 BC	Old Assyrian Period.
1,650 BC	Mycenaean culture begins to flourish on the Greek mainland.
1,640 BC	Conquest of Lower Egypt by the Hyksos.

1,600 BC	End of Nubian C-Group Culture, and end of the Old Babylonian period.
1,595 BC	Capture of Aleppo by the Hittite king Mursili I.
1,560 BC	Accession of the Egyptian king Seqenenre II, who led the Upper Egyptian fight back against the Hyksos.
1,550 BC	Beginning of the New Kingdom Egyptian period.
1,532 BC	Final defeat of the Hyksos by the Egyptian king Ahmose I.
1,500 BC	Egyptian-controlled territory at its greatest extent under the king Thutmose I. Beginning of the Mitanni Kingdom.
1,450 BC	Mycenaeans conquer the Minoans.
1,380 BC	Accession of Hittite king Suppiluliumas I, beginning of the First Syrian War.
1,330 BC	Accession of Ashur-uballit I, beginning of Middle Assyrian period.
1,279 BC	Accession of Ramesses II as Egyptian king.
1,274 BC	Battle of Kadesh.
1,250 BC	Societal collapse of Mycenaean and other eastern Mediterranean cultures.
1,244 BC	Accession of Tukulti-Ninurta I as Assyrian king.
1,231 BC	First record of the arrival of the Sea Peoples.
1,125 BC	Accession of Nebuchadnezzar I of the Fourth Dynasty of Babylon.
1,115 BC	Accession of Tiglath-Pileser I as Assyrian king.
1,080 BC	The Aramaeans invade Mesopotamia.
1,076 BC	End of the Middle Assyrian Empire.
1,069 BC	Beginning of the Egyptian Third Intermediate Period
1,020 BC	Accession of Saul as the king of the United Monarchy.
1,000 BC	Accession of David as the king of the United Monarchy.
961 BC	Accession of Solomon as king of the United Monarchy.
924 BC	The Egyptian king Shoshenq I invades Gaza and Canaan.

911 BC	Adad-nirari II becomes the Assyrian king. Beginning of the Neo-Assyrian Empire.
909 BC	Baasha becomes king of Israel.
885 BC	Assassination of Israelite king Elah by Zimri.
747 BC	Manahem becomes king of Israel.
728 BC	The Neo-Assyrian king Tiglath-Pileser III makes himself the king of Babylon.
720 BC	Assyria invades Israel, leading to its final destruction.
701 BC	Assyria invades Judah, destroying many cities including Lachish. Siege of Jerusalem.
681 BC	Accession of Esarhaddon as Neo-Assyrian king.
668 BC	Accession of Ashurbanipal as the Neo-Assyrian king.
664 BC	Accession of Tanutamun as king of Egypt, beginning of the Egyptian Late Period. Elam invades Babylon.
655 BC	Battle of Ulai River, Ashurbanipal defeats the Elamites.
652 BC	Shamash-shum-ukin leads Babylon and its allies in rebellion against Ashurbanipal.
648 BC	Death of Shamash-shum-ukin, surrender of Babylon to Ashurbanipal.
631 BC	Death or abdication of Ashurbanipal.
626 BC	Rebellion of the Chaldean general called Nabopolassar.
612 BC	Fall of Nineveh to the Medes and Babylonians.
609 BC	Battle of Megiddo.
605 BC	Battle of Carchemish. Accession of Nebuchadnezzar II of Babylon.
604 BC	Capture of Ashkelon by Nebuchadnezzar II.
597 BC	Siege of Jerusalem by Accession of Nebuchadnezzar II.

CHAPTER 1

The Origins of Warfare

When did warfare begin? Conflict has been a permanent feature of human existence, but finding an actual moment in prehistory when we can say it, in fact, started is a complex issue. To find an answer, it is important to define and explain what warfare is. In order to do so, it is necessary to head back 10,000 years to the Neolithic Middle East, where one potential candidate is highlighted to show the very start of warfare. Finally in this chapter, the focus then turns to the arrival of the first complex military systems in the region as the first civilisations arose in Mesopotamian Sumer and Akkad.

What is Warfare?

All *homininae* (humans, chimpanzees, gorillas and their now extinct ancestors) have a propensity for violent action. Human beings are at the extreme end of this spectrum. A number of theories have been put forward to explain this. Many are based on evolutionary benefit in the context of factors such as territorial advantage, reproductive advantage and materialism. The latter, which suggests that conflict is only engaged in when there is some kind of desperate need, is particularly popular at present. An example can be found in the inhabitants of a village suffering from a failed harvest raiding the granaries of their neighbours to survive. But is this warfare? To determine this, a definition needs to be generated.

Some describe warfare as purposeful aggressive action by one group against another involving the use of lethal force. Others argue the word 'group' is too broad a term in this context and say that warfare is aggression of an organised nature between autonomous political units, or polities. This is based on an anthropological model used to define the level of sophistication of a given culture, beginning with band, then progressing to village, then chiefdom and finally state. The first two are egalitarian, while the latter two are stratified, leading to them being called stratified polities. This leads to the question of what organised aggression is. An escalating scale of violence helps here, ranging from homicide, then feuding, next raiding and finally war. The correlation of these two scales therefore provides our axes to give a definition of warfare – the extreme end of organised aggression in the form of war, involving a stratified polity.

Warfare Begins

To establish when warfare began, based on the above definition, we need to turn to the archaeological record. Three types of evidence are particularly useful here:

- Skeletons.
- Mortuary practices, particularly mass burials.
- Material culture, including art, weapons and fortifications.

Evidence for violence between *homininae* is found as far back as 50,000 years ago, for example a *Homo neanderthalensis* skeleton found in the Shanidar Cave, an archaeological site on Bradost Mountain, located in Iraq, featuring a throwing spear puncture wound to a rib. There is then a dramatic rise in evidence for violence between individuals in the European Mesolithic, a period starting 15,000 years ago. Examples include burials at Vedbæk, Denmark, Skateholm, southern Sweden, Stellmoor, Germany, and Vasylivka, Ukraine. All feature wounds caused by a variety of weaponised technologies, such as arrows, axes and maces. Meanwhile, mass graves with similar wounds from sites like the cave sites at el-Arbi and Taforalt in North Africa have been interpreted as evidence of communal violence.

However, none of these examples fit our definition of warfare, given there is no evidence of a stratified polity involved. For that, we have to turn to material culture in the form of fortifications to provide the first evidence of warfare. This can be found in the Pre-Pottery Neolithic A (PPNA) Wall of Jericho on the Jordan River, suggested to date between 8,250 and 7,600 BC.

Jericho was founded around 9,000 BC in the Natufian period, which immediately preceded the Neolithic. This was a time when sedentary hunter-gatherers increasingly remained in one place except on seasonal hunting trips. By the early 9th millennium BC, they had begun to experiment with farming, cultivating wild cereals near to their long-term camps. From this emerged the Neolithic period, with farming spreading in earnest across the Levant. The success of these farming communities led to the coalescence of various families and tribes into larger and larger settlements, leading to the first towns.

The inhabitants of Jericho lived in huts made from mud bricks. This was the ubiquitous building material of the region, its ease of

A typical Tell in the Levant, evidence of centuries of occupation. (John Reid)

use meaning that, as one building collapsed, it was simply levelled and then built over again. Over time, this gave rise to one of the most common sights when looking for biblical locations in the Levant: noticeable mounds called *tells* in Hebrew, *hüyük* in Turkish, and *tepe* in Persian.

The people in Jericho lived on domesticated emmer wheat, barley, figs and pulses. Goats, gazelle and wild sheep added to the diet. However, the success of the settlement was not down to its agricultural prowess. Jericho's location is actually in a rather hot and arid locale near the Dead Sea. Rather, its rise to prominence came about because it became a crucial emporium at the end of a long-range trading network reaching hundreds of miles north to mountainous Anatolia. This was the source of the very high-quality obsidian with which the region's finest tools were made. Large quantities of the material were sent south to Jericho on caravans, which in return supplied Dead Sea minerals to its northerly trading partners. These were the luxury goods of their day, and over time Jericho's control of the southern end of this trade route made it very wealthy. By the time the first walls were built, it had grown to 2.4 hectares in size, with a population of 1,500. This was larger than the much more famous later Bronze Age town, referenced in Chapter 5.

Jericho's regional affluence soon began to attract the unwelcomed attention of desert raiders, to the extent that its very survival was threatened. It is in this context that its first wall circuit was built, the intention being to turn the town into a fortified trading outpost. The scale of these free-standing stone walls is striking, being 600m in length, up to 4m high, up to 2m thick, and featuring an 8.5m high conical tower with an integral stone-built staircase. This level of engineering skill at such an early date is astonishing, requiring a huge level of societal commitment to complete. One estimate argues it would have taken 10,400 man-days to complete the circuit and tower alone. Additionally, a defensive ditch was then dug outside the wall 8.2m wide and 2.7m deep, cut through solid bedrock. The whole construction project shows a very high level of political organisation, and certainly indicates that there was a stratified polity at work. Further, this defensive network was clearly built for a military purpose, and so it can be argued that this wall circuit is the first evidence of what we can call warfare.

Sumer

Mesopotamia, the historical area defining the rivers systems of the Tigris and Euphrates in modern Syria, Iraq and Kuwait, is often called the cradle of civilisation. In a western context, intensive agriculture, mass industrial production, urbanism and national government all began here. The region didn't rise to prominence immediately, however, with the next stages of the development in farming and material culture occurring at its northern and western fringes in the Zagros mountains and eastern Anatolia, where reliable rainfall was to be found. It was here that the first pigs were domesticated, bread wheat cultivated, flax grown to make linen, and from 7,000 BC pottery made for the first time.

However, it was on the fertile floodplains of Mesopotamia that we find the first evidence of true urban living. Farming settlements started to spread south there from around 6,800 BC, and by 5,500 BC they were found across the whole region. Successive cultures briefly flowered, each identifiable by their types of pottery. The Hassuna of northern Mesopotamia from 6,500 to 6,000 BC, was the first to make painted pottery and also to use stamp seals to record transactions. They were replaced here by the Halafian culture. However, it was the Samarrans to their south, also flourishing from around 6,000 BC, who first made true urban living possible. That was because they invented the first large-scale irrigation techniques, including the building of canals. This proved vital in boosting yields in some of the less fertile land, especially in southern Mesopotamia. There, from 5,900 BC, a culture known as the Ubaid lasted for 1,500 years, with the invention of the plough further improving yields. By the 5th millennium BC, true towns such as Eridu, with religious centres, had emerged here, with the Ubaid culture replacing the Halafian's to their north by 5,400 BC. They were therefore the first culture to dominate the entire region. Their dominance of the long-range trading networks used to procure raw materials to their north and west, and even down the Persian Gulf, aided their success. Further, their invention of an accounting system based on clay tokens helped them manage the trade. This was effectively the beginning of writing. There is no evidence that warfare played a role in this expansion, likely as it was. It was certainly a key feature of the culture that followed the Sumerians.

With this new culture we can talk for the first time of civilisation. The period of Sumerian dominance featured the rise of powerful cities with highly centralised governments (vital to maintain the irrigation systems that allowed their growing populations to be fed), stratified societies with social classes, formal state religion, well organised trading networks and – for the first time in this narrative – armies. The inhabitants of the cities in southern Mesopotamia were native to the region and spoke Sumerian, while those in the north spoke Akkadian, a Semitic language. This was to prove a key point of difference later.

The first phase of Sumerian expansion is named after the oldest and largest city, Uruk. This period lasted from 4,300 BC to 3,100 BC. As this stage progressed, cities grew in size to feature populations of up to 10,000. The key ones formed competing city-states, with the capital ringed by outlying towns and villages. Examples included Ur, Eridu, Lagash, Nippur and Kish, the latter in Akkad to the north. The Uruk Period was a time of growth and prosperity (at least for the elites in society), but from 2,900 BC this was replaced by the much more problematic Early Dynastic Period. This lasted until 2,334 BC and was a period when all the major cities built huge defensive wall circuits. Some cities grew to an enormous size, with Uruk's population growing to 50,000 and its city walls enclosing an area of 6.2 square kilometres. Epigraphy and the archaeological record are insightful here, showing true state versus state warfare, often endemic at this time. This was driven by the need to control the long-range supply routes through which the rapidly growing city-states were supplied with building stone, good quality wood and metal ores. These were vital natural resources that were scarce locally. This reliance on vital long-range imports also left supply routes vulnerable to interdiction and raiding by neighbouring peoples. These included the Elamites in modern western Iran (with its famous capital at Susa), the Guti in the Zagros Mountains and the Bedouin Martu in the near-eastern desert.

The main city-state rivalries for most of the Early Dynastic Period were between Uruk, Kish and Ur. The most famous battle of this period was at Uruk, in 2,600 BC, when its king, the famous Gilgamesh, led a rebellion against the overlordship of Kish, capturing seven 'heroes of Kish' in the engagement. The ongoing tripartite rivalry between the three city-states (both Ur and Kish were themselves conquered by King Mesannepadda of Ur in 2,500 BC) was brought to a dramatic end towards the end of the period by the unlikely conquest of Sumer by the Elamites. The Sumerian revival was led by Kish, and from that point on until the rise of Akkad under Sargon the Great in 2,334 BC. Regional dominance frequently switched between the other city-states, including Lagash and then Umma.

The cities of Sumer were complex institutions that shared many common features. At the centre of each was a religious complex that acted as the main administrative centre, organising trade and employing thousands of workers on the land and in state workshops. This complex often featured a raised religious platform, the precursor to the later ziggurats. Such was the importance of these structures that many city-states considered themselves the property of their patron God. Early on, this led to many Sumerian rulers styling themselves as the *En* (lord) or *Ensi* (governor) of their patron deities' 'earthly estate'. Later, a third title for ruler emerged, a *Lugal* (great man), who reigned over a number of city-states. This reflected the increasing sophistication of Sumerian civilisation, as improved communications through state-built roads and along waterways facilitated political control over larger and larger areas. The ultimate prize for an overlord was control over Nippur and Kish. The former was the definitive holy city given it was 'home' to Enlil, the supreme God of the Sumerian pantheon, while the latter had from an early date been associated with dominance across Sumer, the 'King of Kish' becoming synonymous with supreme overlordship.

Most of the populations in these city-states were landless labourers and tenants called *Erin*, a word derived from the Sumerian for 'yoke', indicating their lowly place in society. The majority were employed on religious and royal estates, which between them accounted for around two thirds of the overall land composition of each city-state. Even at this most basic level of society the degree of organisation is evident, with some of the most common words in the increasingly sophisticated written record (archaic proto-cuneiform appears from the late 4th millennia BC) reflecting levels of workforce supervision. These included *Agrig* (superintendents), *Sanga* (stewards), *Ugala* (commanders) and *Nu-Banda* (captains). The military connotations of the latter two are relevant. This is because it is likely that the ability of the early Sumerian kings to raise their newly structured armies was derived from the societal organisation necessary to run the religious and royal estates and maintain the densely organised Sumerian irrigation network.

In times of conflict the ruler of a given city-state relied on two classes of warrior. The first were household troops called *Shub-lugal* (King's retainer), with the small city-state of Shuruppak providing insight from a time when it was subject to control by nearby and much larger Nish. Here, written records from 2,600 BC highlight a royal household of over 600 men, including 144 cup bearers and 113 musicians. These titles are most likely honorific, reflecting the holder's status as a royal retainer. The second class of soldier was the *Aga-Ush* (follower). These could comprise both *Erin*, regularly employed in the military as part of their commitment to the city-state, and others conscripted from their regular roles in civilian

A Sumerian army ready for battle. (James Hamilton)

employ on religious and royal estates. The latter featured most prominently in larger armies.

Military units had fixed sizes, with a *Nu-Banda* commanding between 60 to 100 men, dependent on the city-state. Larger units were formed from brigading together such formations, with the largest such company based on written records coming from Shuruppak and numbering 680 men.

Most early Sumerian troops were armed with bows, according to Archaic proto-cuneiform texts dating to the late 4th millennium BC. These list large bodies of archers under military officers, with side arms including hand axes and sickle-swords. This was perhaps the first regular army. Later, we then have some fabulous artefacts dating to the Early Dynastic Period in the archaeological record that provide detailed illustrations of the evolution of Sumerian armies into a completely different kind of fighting force. Such artefacts include a lyre from the Royal cemetery at Ur, with a sound bow depicting scenes from a battle in the mid-3rd millennium BC. The illustrations, lovingly crafted in lapis lazuli and shell, show elite warriors in what are now termed battle-cars, and ordered ranks spearmen wielding their two-handed weapons. The latter have copper alloy or leather helmets and wear ankle-length long cloaks that appear to be covered in defensive-copper alloy discs. Another famous artefact is the so-called Stele of the Vultures, an upper and lower sequence of illustrations on a stone slab from the middle-ranking city-state of Lagash. This also shows battle-chariots, the king riding in one, and well-ordered ranks of spearmen. This find may date to a slightly later period as the spearmen, still wearing the same helmets and again carrying two-handed spears as depicted on the lyre from Ur, are now show with (at least in the front rank) very large and clumsy looking rectangular body shields in their front rank. As to the cloaks on the spearmen on the lyre, these are also covered in

Sumerian battle cars ready for war. (James Hamilton)

what seem to be copper alloy discs. A final item to consider here is the golden helmet of the Sumerian king Meskalamdug, again from the Royal cemetery at Ur. This has beautifully crafted curled hair, the precious representation held in place by a bun at the back. This is exactly the same design as that worn by the king on the Stele of the Vultures, including the decorated earpieces.

Taken together, this and other evidence shows that Sumerian military tactics and technology had developed vastly from the late-4th millennium BC. One has the *Shub-lugal* (household troops) riding to war in for-that-time highly sophisticated battle cars. These were fighting platforms rather than shock weapons. They featured four small wagon-like solid wheels and steep sides up to chest height at the front and above the fore-wheels, these reduced to knee-length above the rear wheels. Across the front quivers of throwing spears can be seen (they may represent javelins, but look large on the images which are otherwise anatomically well balanced). Each has

A Sumerian spearman's phalanx. (James Hamilton)

a crew of two, one the driver holding long leather straps attached to a yoke, and the other a warrior. Given the fact that some of the latter hold long hand axes, it may well be they remained in the battle cars while throwing their missile weapons, then fought on foot as with later Homeric and Gallic charioteers. Four equids pulled the battle cars, indicating their bulk. The animals could have been domesticated asses called *Anshe*, mules called *Anshe-Bar-An*, or a further crossbreed. True horses, attested for this period as *Ansh-Shul-Gi*, are not shown in a military context and were perhaps too expensive to risk in conflict. In terms of the numbers fielded by each city-state, Umma is said to have been able to field 60. Meanwhile, smaller platform and straddle cars are also shown in contemporary illustrations, light versions of the above with one crew, and drawn by two equids. These, together with a very limited number of equid-mounted true cavalry, may have performed a scouting and communications function.

The massed ranks of spearmen are equally enigmatic in the illustrations and epigraphy. They clearly show the very high level of societal organisation available to mid and later Sumerian leaders, allowing these troops to fight in deep phalanxes of warriors carrying long two-handed spears. The presence of state-level organisation is also very evident in their uniform appearance, as they all wear the same ubiquitous helmet and clothes. Further, the advance of military technology through the experience of war is also evident in the progression of the defensive panoply of the spearmen, the earlier ones having the long cloak and later troops the body shield, at least in the front rank. As with the much later Greek city-states and their development of phalanx-based warfare, this perhaps shows the result of inter city-state conflict. In this context, each sought to learn from their experiences in order to generate a tactical advantage over their neighbours.

Side arms for these troops would again have been hand axes and sickle-swords, with the new addition of the dagger. Maces are also commonly depicted, but very rarely, and usually in the context of officers. In terms of the quality of these spearmen, while most would be *Aga-Ush*, the presence of *Shub-lugal* to stiffen the ranks cannot be ruled out, or even to provide indigenous elite spear-armed guard units.

Sumerian armies of this period also featured specialist troops to support the main army in the field. This might be in the form of lightly armed rough terrain warriors with short spears and javelins, or skirmishing bowmen (slingers and javelin-men are rarely depicted). These were often recruited from neighbouring peoples, either as mercenaries or allies. A final comment here is that there appears to be no depiction of siege warfare of any kind, with all the engagements shown being set-piece battles. This seems unusual given most major cities featured huge city walls and may show that offensive military technology had yet to catch up with the defensive technology of the time.

Akkad

Sumerian dominance of Mesopotamia was brought to a shuddering halt by the world's first great conqueror, Sargon the Great. Such was his success he became one of the most revered rulers in the ancient near east, his name a paradigm for military success, even earning the title 'King of Battles'.

Sargon was of lowly birth in Kish, his father a date grower. He rose to prominence through a career in the military, eventually becoming a cupbearer to the king. In 2,334 BC he led a successful revolt against his master, becoming ruler himself. As a usurper, he knew the value of military success and quickly set about a series of wars of conquest, first against the other Semitic-speaking Akkadian cities, and then targeting the rich Sumerian cities to the south. There, resistance to his aggression was led by Lugalzagesi, king of both of Uruk and Umma. Three huge battles followed, with Sargon the eventual victor. We have detail of the final one, the Sumerians gathering an enormous army containing the troops of 50 *Ensi* (governors). Sargon defeated them nevertheless, with Lugalzagesi captured and displayed in a neck-stock on the Enlil Gate of Kish back in Akkad. Such was the price of defeat in ancient Mesopotamia.

Overall, Sargon fought and won 34 battles in his war against the Sumerian city-states. This included the sacking of Umma, Lagash and Ur. He then 'washed his weapons' in the waters of the Persian Gulf to signal his dominion over the whole of Sumer and Akkad. To ensure the loyalty of the newly conquered Sumerian city-states, he then replaced all of their rulers with his own Akkadian supporters, the new governors called *shakkanakum*. He also ensured the loyalty of the powerful religious classes in each city by appointing his own daughter, Enheduanna, as the high priestess of the powerful moon God Nanna in Ur. In a long reign that lasted until his death in 2,279 BC, he went on to conquer Syria all the way to the Mediterranean coast (perhaps even Cyprus), eastern Anatolia, parts of Elam in modern Iran, and even the trading emporium island of Dilmun (modern Bahrain) in the Persian Gulf. Some suggest his rule there extended even further south to Oman.

Numerous writings record Sargon's victorious reign. Key to his success was the legal unification of all the differing ethnicities in his mighty empire. He also built a brand-new capital city, Agade, near modern Babylon. Akkadian supremacy reached its height under Sargon's grandson Naram-Sin, who reigned from 2,254 to 2,218 BC, but the empire was always prone to frequent revolts given its vast size, including the Sumerian Great Revolt of 2,250 BC. By 2,193 BC the Akkadian Empire had collapsed, caused by a region-wide revolt led by the Semitic-speaking Amorites of Syria (see Chapters 2 and 3 for detail), and invasions from the north by the Gutians of the Zagros Mountains.

In terms of military developments during the period of Akkadian control in Mesopotamia, the military establishment was still dominated by the combination of battle cars (less so as time progressed, given the far-reaching nature of the campaigning) and spearmen phalanxes. Sargon's own household of 5,400 at his palace at Agade included many *Shub-lugal* (household troops), who formed the core of his field armies, both manning the battle cars and leading the spearmen. He also introduced a new tier in the household hierarchy called *Sagi-mah* (chief cup bearer). This may be the title given to his generals. Another innovation was the creation of a new class of soldier called the *niskum*. These troops were given plots of land by the king, together with additional rations of fish and salt. This was the first attempt at maintaining a full-time standing army, these semi-professionals being at the king's call whenever required. We also now have a name for the skirmishing troops of the day, who are called *Nim* (flies). These were armed for the first time with the composite bow, a big technological advance using laminated horn, wood and sinew instead of wood alone, which dramatically improved the penetrating power of the arrows.

Additionally, we also have detail of the organisation of the Akkadian soldiery, whether *Shub-lugal, niskum* or *Aga-Ush*. This is in the form of their bread ration, issued in lots of 30, 60, 90, 120, 180, 240 and 600 loaves (the same as with workmen on the religious and royal estates). This indicates multiples of 60 men to a unit, with a subdivision of 30. For example, Sargon's household of 5,400 would represent nine 'regiments' of 600 men. Finally, anecdote suggests Akkadian mastery of siege warfare given to Sargon was clearly very successful in assaulting the extremely well-protected cities of Sumer.

Third Dynasty of Ur

After the fall of Akkad, Mesopotamia resorted to independent city-state rule once more, this lasting for 80 years. Then, in 2,112 BC, a Sumerian renaissance followed with the accession of Ur-Nammu, the first king of the Third Dynasty of Ur. In a reign lasting until 2,095 BC, he rebuilt a Sumerian empire stretching as far north as Assyria. Crucially, this was through diplomacy as much as force, with regional peace and stability seeing a great flowering of art and culture. One manifestation was the appearance for the first time of the ziggurat in the city-state religious complexes. This development of the existing raised religious platform was a terraced compound of successively receding levels made from locally made bricks and imported stone, with a shrine at the top. The first were built at Ur, Eridu, Uruk and Nippur.

The Third Dynastic period remained stable until 2,034 BC when nomadic Aramite peoples started raiding deep into the Empire from the Syrian desert. Then, in 2,004 BC, a huge Elamite invasion from the north destroyed all before it. Soon Ur itself was sacked and the dynasty fell. The next two hundred years saw yet again the city-states exerting their independence, increasingly under Amorite cultural influence. This led to the emergence of Assyria and Babylon, two new super-powers that were to dominate the region for next millennia and more.

The main military innovation of the kings of the Third Dynasty of Ur was organisational, and at the top tier of government. Mindful of the frequent rebellions during the Akkadian period, from this time, the *Ensi* (governors) in charge of each city-state lost their authority over the regional military, this then becoming the responsibility of a new post called the *Shakkana*. This was of equal status to an *Ensi*, the twin positions analogously being very similar to the much later Roman system of running a province through a procurator and a governor. Again, we also see here how military organisation replicated that in civilian life in the region at the time, with the *Shakkana* also responsible for the conscription of labourers on religious and royal estates.

CHAPTER 2

Egypt, Nubia, Canaan and Libya

Civilisation, and warfare associated with it, also occurred at the south-western end of the Fertile Crescent contemporaneously with that in Mesopotamia. Here, the River Nile played the crucial role in the development of ancient Egypt, Nubia to its south, Canaan to its north and Libya to its west. Each is discussed in turn in this chapter.

Egypt

As mentioned in the introduction, the full story of later ancient Egyptian warfare is considered in a sister Casemate title. However, it is an important part of the wider story of warfare in the Old Testament period. Therefore, given the crucial parallels with the development of warfare in Mesopotamia, the origins of military activity in Egypt are discussed here with a focus on Pre-Dynastic (6,000–3,150 BC), Early Dynastic (3,150–2, 686 BC) and Old Kingdom Egypt (2,686–2,134 BC). Subsequent events in the Middle and New Kingdom are then referenced at the end of this section in terms of later military developments and, regarding events, in later chapters.

The River Nile is physically defined by a series of cataracts. These are shallow lengths in the river creating white water rapids. There are six overall ranging north to south, but it is the first that is most important here. This is located at Aswan, today some 840km as the crow flies from the Mediterranean coastline of the Nile Delta.

From that cataract through to this vast delta, the Nile flows through a narrow valley, never more than a few kilometres wide and often less. The river, trapped in this narrow confine for much of the year, then spectacularly floods in late summer each year, leaving the flood plains covered in fresh silt. Some argue that these flood plains, which stay moist throughout the winter months, were the most fertile land in the ancient world.

Farming began in this verdant valley and on its flood plains around 6,000 BC, with Neolithic settlements emerging throughout the region soon after. Steady population growth followed and by 4,000 BC the valley was heavily settled with subsistence farmers. By 3,300 BC the first towns had appeared, their populations coalescing around the political leadership needed to maximise the potential of the agricultural gifts of the Nile. In particular, canals came into use to allow the floodwaters to reach previously uncultivated land, with storehouses then appearing to stock the surpluses made possible by the very high yields. This provided a cushion to mitigate against any harvest shocks if the Nile failed to flood, giving stability to the regional settlement. Crucially, it also provided the extra food needed to feed newly emerging classes in society, including administrators, merchants, craftsmen, priests and – for the first time in the region – soldiers.

Competition between the settlements in the Nile Valley was intense, and they gradually amalgamated into larger and larger political units. Soon there were just two, Upper Egypt below Aswan and Lower Egypt above it.

Around 3,000 BC, Narmer, king of Upper Egypt, conquered Lower Egypt to the north and became the first ruler over the entire valley. He was therefore the first Early Dynastic Egyptian king (locally styled pharaoh), and founder of the first Egyptian dynasty. Narmer founded Memphis, south of the Nile Delta, as the capital of his newly unified kingdom, this benefiting economically from the invention of hieroglyphic writing around this time. This pictogram-based system had evolved from the symbolic motifs used to decorate pottery, with an early example of its use appearing on the slate pallets carved to record Narmer's victories. Such epigraphy showed a mature and flourishing political system based on theocratic kingship.

The political institutions of Egypt continued to develop into the second dynasty of the Early Dynastic period, with a steadily improving state administration progressively increasing royal power. This provided the stability for the four dynasties which then dominated the region during the Old Kingdom period. Under the first two, the third and fourth in the overall sequence of Egyptian dynasties, Egypt flourished. However, during the fifth and sixth dynasties the monarchy was weakened when it increased the granting out of key positions in government and land to the nobility as a reward for loyal service. Those particularly favoured, soon began to make their own posts hereditary. These roles then gradually drifted out of royal control. At the same time, the River Nile was hit by a series of low floods, seriously damaging annual crop yields. Starvation followed, and eventually the Old Kingdom collapsed. Egypt was then divided once more into Lower and Upper Egypt in the First Intermediate Period, before a renaissance with the onset of the Middle Kingdom.

Government in Early Dynastic and Old Kingdom Egypt was centralised around the royal household. The highest state official was called the *vizier* who administered taxation and justice. Beneath him were a series of chancellors, store controllers and other officials, all supported by highly skilled scribes trained in writing, mathematics and astronomy. From this centrality, power was devolved down to a series of regional provinces called *nomes*, 20 in Lower Egypt and 22 in Upper Egypt. Each was run by a governor called a *Haty-a* or *nomarch*. It was these officials in particular who, as detailed above, were to become so troublesome towards the end of the Old Kingdom.

As with Mesopotamia, religion was at the centre of life in ancient Egypt. The kings continued to be theocrats, earthly representatives of the well-known Egyptian pantheon. They were believed by their subjects to be of divine descent and immortal. Therefore, as part of the funerary process, great attention was paid to the perseveration of their bodies when they died. Early royal tombs, crammed with the luxuries of everyday elite living, were built on platforms called *mastabas*. These were superseded by the famous pyramids from the reign of King Djoser of the Third Dynasty who reigned from 2,668 BC to 2,649 BC. His 62-metre tall funerary platform is known as the Step Pyramid and was constructed at the ancient burial grounds at Saqqara. Pyramid building climaxed around 2,550 BC with the construction of the 146-metre high Great Pyramid constructed for Khufu, second king of the Fourth Dynasty.

Military activity during the Early Dynastic and Old Kingdom periods was usually in the context of four main causes. These were raiding by Nubian tribes anywhere south of the first cataract at Aswan, raiding by the Canaanites to the north, and raiding from the west by Libyan tribes, and also internal conflict between individual *nomes* or in civil wars. In regards to the first three, the usual Egyptian

The Giza pyramid complex at Giza, ancient Egyptian funerary monumentalism from the Old Kingdom period. (Wikimedia Commons)

response was a savage punitive counter-invasion deep into enemy territory once the raid had been contained. The Nubian threat in the south also provoked an innovative response in the form of a long chain of forts, some very large, built up the Nile from Aswan. Many of these are now underwater in Lake Nasser. When in use, they acted as a deterrent against Nubian aggression and, given most appear to have never been attacked, seem to have been successful.

There was no professional army in Egypt during this period. Instead, the governor of each *nome* had to raise his own volunteer army in time of conflict. Military service was not considered prestigious and, therefore, the gathered military units were usually composed of men from the lower classes of society. The general reserve of young men who were eligible for recruitment by a *nomarch* was called the *djamu*, having a limited term of service. The main body of these were called *hewenu-nefru* (the youthful recruits), led by a cadre of seasoned soldiers called *ahautyu* (warriors) who wore red ostrich plumes, and whose role may have been hereditary, a son replacing a father in the *nomarch*'s service. These were likely a throwback to pre-dynastic Egypt, the most experienced called *menfat* (shock troops). The latter had their own commanders, called *imy-er menfat*. The king and *nomarch*'s most highly trained troops were their own retainers, called *shemsu*.

For a national campaign, the king would call on each relevant *nomarch*, depending on the geography of the campaigning region, to raise and supply a contingent for the army to serve under the overall command of the king. Each *nomarch* served as his contingent's commander and could even operate as an independent general if tasked by the king with a specific role in a campaign. The size of each contingent was dependent on the size and population density of the *nomes*, ranging from around 300 warriors to 1,000. *Nomarchs* could also be given additional roles in the king's army, for example the *nomarchic* title *imy-er aw*, meaning 'scout leader' or 'commander of foreign auxiliaries'. The latter is instructive, showing the king and his *nomarchs* bolstering their armies with foreign troops, for example Nubians when campaigning in the south, Canaanites in the north and Libyans in the west. The tasks given to the *nomarch* by the king might also be civilian in nature, for example, quarrying the vast quantities of stone needed for the Egyptian built environment or the construction of pyramids.

The flexibility of the system of brigading each *nomarch*'s warrior contingent into a campaigning army, supported by auxiliaries, could prove a source of instability in times of weak central control, allowing individual *nomarchs* to act as independent warlords. This was particularly the case during the Fifth and Sixth Dynasties at the end of the Old Kingdom, when some *nomarchs* began to make their posts hereditary as detailed above. We have a specific example of a *nomarch* acting as a warlord in the First Intermediate Period, when a governor called Ankhtify of a *nome* known as Nekhen (also called Hierakonpolis) in Upper Egypt, united the forces of three *nomes* to campaign under his command during this particularly anarchic period.

One alternative means for a king gathering an army is also mentioned. This involved the monarch sending a scribe to each of the *nomes* to select one man in a hundred to gather under his banner as *henu-nefru* (household recruits) in a royal army built around his own *shemsu* retainers. The whole was commanded by an *imy-er henu-nefru* (commander of the household recruits) general. However, the *nomarchic* system of the king brigading each *nomarch*'s forces into a single homogenous army, seems to have been much more common.

Naval power was also important in Early Dynastic and Old Kingdom Egypt. This is no surprise given the vital importance of the River Nile to all levels of ancient Egyptian society. Naval force could also be used in the Mediterranean, and there is a specific example from the reign of King Pepi I during the Sixth Dynasty. This was the battle of the Antelope's Nose, when the king's general, Weni, a highly regarded strategist of his day, engaged an army of nomadic tribesmen in southern Canaan. Here, he divided his army into two, the first force heading north by land to pin the enemy in place, while the second was transported by sea to land to the enemy's rear. Both forces then engaged their opponents from both directions, the trapped tribesmen being wiped out.

Troops of all kinds in Early Dynastic and Old Kingdom Egypt were equipped from central state-run arsenals, reflecting the structured nature of the society by that time. One was located in Lower Egypt, and another in Upper Egypt. The warriors were equipped either as bowmen with a simple single-arched bow, or as close-fighting troops. The latter were armed with axes, short spears called *dja*, cudgels called *ames*, fighting staves, maces (usually associated with officers) and daggers called *ta-agsu*. *Menfat* and *shemsu* are often depicted wielding particularly hefty axes, for example the eye-axe, which could be used one- or two-handed. For defensive equipment, the close-fighting troops carried a shield called an *ikem* made from planked wood covered with bull-hide. These could range in size from covering the torso, to being a full body shield. The archers had no defensive equipment. Only the officers seem to have worn helmets, made from leather, copper or various kinds of copper alloy.

In terms of battle array, the archers and close-fighting warriors were deployed in separate deep columns, either intermingled across the battle line (an archer formation followed by a close-fighting formation and so on), or with the close-fighting troops in the centre and archers on the wings. Auxiliaries were then deployed to protect the flanks and to skirmish ahead. The standard tactic was to reduce the enemy with bow fire before the close-fighting troops engaged, the bowmen usually trying to stay away from any close combat.

From a military perspective, later periods of ancient Egyptian history fall broadly in four phases, namely the Middle Kingdom from the end of the First Intermediate Period in 2055 BC until 1,650 BC, then the Second Intermediate Period until 1,550 BC (which included much of the period of Hyksos domination of Lower Egypt through to 1,527 BC, see Chapter 3), next the New Kingdom until 1,069 BC, then the Third Intermediate Period until 664 BC (including the Libyan, Kushite and part of the Saitic sub-periods), and finally in terms of this work a Late Period until 332 BC. Given the armies of the Middle Kingdom were broadly similar to those of the Old Kingdom, and those of the Third Intermediate and Late Periods increasingly fall out of the scope of this work, here I detail in brief the army of the New Kingdom.

Early in this period the Egyptian army was split into two corps, under the overall command of the Pharaoh supported by his Vizier who served as his Minister of War. One corps was positioned in the north and one the south, this based on the earlier system of state-run arsenals of the Early Dynastic and Old/Middle Kingdoms. They were later increased in number to three, these now called Amun, P're and Ptah after the patron gods of the regions they were based in, these being Thebes, Heliopolis and Memphis. Later a fourth corps called Seth was added, this based on the patron god of the then-new capital city Pi-Ramesses. Each corps had responsibility to provide field armies when the Pharaoh was on campaign, for example at Kadesh under Ramesses II. Such field armies were commanded by a general called an *imy-er mesha*, with his assistants called *idnu*.

By this time the elite troops in the Egyptian army were the chariotry, of the nimble two-horsed and composite bow-armed variety. The vector of their introduction into Egypt is discussed in detail in Chapter 3 in the context of the advent of the *maryannu*. The Egyptians called their chariots *ta-net-hetry*, with each crewed by a *kedjen* (driver) who multi-tasked as a shield-bearer, and a *seneny* (archer). The cab of these highly manoeuvrable chariots was 1m in width and 1.25m in height, with a 2.5m long draught pole, an axle width of 1.75m and six-spoked wheels 90cm in diameter. Two weapons cases either side of the cab carried a large number of arrows, allowing the *seneny* to maintain a high rate of fire against opponents. The two horses were often armoured with textile trappers covered in bronze or leather scales. Egyptian chariots were often accompanied by *peherer* (chariot runners) who fought alongside on foot. A *kedjen-tepy* (junior officer) commanded a troop of 10 chariots, with five such troops forming a squadron. These could then be brigaded together in larger units of up to 250. Individual squadrons often had imaginative names, for example Manifest-in-Justice and The Phoenix. The elite chariots in the army were those manned by the nobility (their *seneny* also sometimes armed with a short spear), and particularly those of the pharaoh's guard. It is noteworthy that the pharaoh himself also fought in a chariot, with many incumbents so depicted on reliefs from across the ancient Egyptian world. By this time New Kingdom Egyptian armies also featured a small cavalry component, these scouts called *khapityu* who were armed with a bow and sometimes wore padded textile armour.

However, the main component of New Kingdom Egyptian armies remained heavy infantry, again in the form of bowmen (now called *megau*, or 'shooters') and spearmen (now called *nakthu-a*, or 'strong arm-boys'), once more deployed in separate formations. The basic formation was the *sa* of 250 men, with two or more forming a *pedjet* (host). Each company had its own standard carried by the *tjai-seryt* (standard bearer), and many also had evocative names, for example Pacifier of Gods, Strong in Valour and Bull in Nubia.

In terms of equipment, the foot archers of New Kingdom Egyptian armies carried as standard the composite bow, introduced into Egypt during the period of Hyksos domination of Lower Egypt. This was double-convex in appearance when unstrung, but once strung took the triangular form familiar in many ancient Egyptian reliefs dating to this period. Such bows were up to 1.3m long and comprised laminated strips of wood, horn and sinew. Arrows were made from reed or hardwood, and tipped with bronze arrow-heads. Better-off archers also carried a side-arm, though most were unprotected. Meanwhile the *nakthu-a* were often equipped in a similar manner to their Old and Middle Kingdom predecessors, for example with the *dja* (short spear, though these were now often longer) and two-handed axes. Their shields were now larger, and many now wore body armour of various kinds. Both foot troop types often wore striped head cloths throughout the period.

A final innovation as the New Kingdom progressed was the introduction into Egyptian armies of regular, allied and mercenary units of 'foreign' line-of-battle troops. Early on these included Syro-Canaanite *maryannu* and Gasgan foot troops from the Zagros Mountains. Later Sea Peoples (see Chapter 4) and Libyan units of foot troops were added.

Nubia

Nubia was the region along the River Nile between the first cataract at Aswan and, heading upriver, Khartoum above the sixth cataract where the White and Blue Niles join. It was historically divided into two parts, Wawat (or Lower Nubia) from Aswan to the second cataract south of Wadi Halfa, and Kush (or upper Nubia) above this. The river valley as it travels through the former is very narrow and only supported a small population in the period covered, with the scrublands and desert to the west, and east inhabited by nomadic tribesmen. This section often formed part of Upper Egypt. However, Kush to the south had very fertile flood plains and was densely populated.

Egypt campaigned in Nubia from the time of the First Dynasty in the Early Dynastic Period, aiming to exploit the raw materials in the region and open up the southerly trade route with Africa. The first Nubians they encountered are known as the A-Group, who had a culture similar to Pre-Dynastic Egypt. This survived through to

Nubian warriors. (Simon Clarke)

around 2,800 BC. By the time of the Sixth Dynasty, they had been superseded by the C-Group culture, with individual tribes now being named for the first time. These included the Irtjet, Medjay, Wawat, Yam, Setju and Kaau, all often at war with each other, and frequently providing Egypt with auxiliary troops. This culture lasted from 2,500 BC through to 1,600 BC. Also, from 2,500 BC, further south, a large kingdom arose, named after its capital city of Kerma, famous for its cemetery of over 30,000 graves. Later, the Kingdom of Kush arose here which proved to be a significant threat to Egypt during the Middle and New Kingdom periods.

The majority of warriors in Nubian armies were unarmoured bowmen using a simple self-bow. They were highly skilled with this and proved popular auxiliaries and allies in Early Dynastic and Old Kingdom Egyptian armies. Elite troops and officers were armed with various melee weapons, including axes and maces. Nubians were renowned skirmishers who avoided close combat if possible, with the later Middle Kingdom king Senusret III, complaining they ran away when he attacked and attacked when he withdrew.

Nubian command group. (Simon Clarke)

Canaan

This was a Semitic-speaking region during the 3rd and 2nd millenniums BC and the land Abraham headed to from Haran in Chapter 12 of the Book of Genesis. It broadly corresponded with the area between the Levantine Mediterranean coast, up to the modern Syrian border and, going inland, the Dead Sea, Jordan River and Sea of Galilee.

The name Canaan is derived from the Akkadian *kinakhkhu*. This means 'reddish purple' and is thought to reference the Tyrian Purple dye industry there, later made famous as a Phoenician export, which used the secretions produced by predatory sea snails. Canaanite is a catch-all term used for all of the tribes and peoples of this region, often being referenced in many other Old Testament stories of the Bible.

The region was divided into two at this time, a more advanced north featuring a number of major cities, including the famous Sodom and Gomorrah, which were founded as early as 3,500 BC, and a less settled south where nomadic tribes predominated. The north was a land of plenty, according to contemporary sources, the Egyptian story of the court official Sinuhe, dating to the early 2nd

Canaanite axe blade from the early 2nd millennium BC. (The Metropolitan Museum of Art, Rogers Fund, 1961)

Hilly terrain in Canaan, more difficult passage for the armies of the period. (John Reid)

The Dead Sea at sunset. (John Reid)

The coastline of the Dead Sea. (John Reid)

century BC, saying it was abundant in barley, emmer wheat, figs and fruits of all types, honey, olives and vines. The tale says the latter were so widespread that wine was more common there than water. However, the land became progressively inhospitable and arid as one headed south, excepting along the Mediterranean coast and in the valley of the Jordan River. The northerly cities used ports along the Mediterranean coast to trade with Anatolia and Egypt, particularly in timber from modern Lebanon and bitumen and minerals from the Dead Sea region. These cities were able to put armies of significant size in the field, for example, as referenced in the Book of Genesis, when Sodom and Gomorrah led a coalition of regional cities against a Mesopotamian army. It is unclear if this was Sumerian or Akkadian, though certainly the cities in the far north of Canaan increasingly came under Mesopotamian cultural influence. As time progressed, some of these became increasingly advanced, for example, Ebla in modern Syria that was organised along Sumerian lines.

The Dead Sea, barren terrain for Biblical campaigning. (Steve Tibble)

Egypt campaigned throughout Canaan at different times. Many Canaanite city-states in the north and tribes in the south are referenced in Egyptian execration texts, magical curses placed on their enemies by the Egyptians. Gradually, however, Amorite influence spread southwards from around 2,400 BC. These were another Semitic-speaking people, originating from the Jebel Bishri mountainous region in northern Syria who migrated southwards. They were prompted to do so by a long-term drought in their homeland caused by climate change. As they travelled south, they took on many of the manifestations of Mesopotamian culture, and, once in northern Canaan, established their own powerful city-states that replaced those of their indigenous Canaanite rivals. Examples, dating from the beginning of the 2nd millennium BC, included Yamhad in northern Syria, and Qatna to its south. It was a federation of Amorite and native Canaanite princes that founded the Hyksos Empire, discussed in Chapter 3.

Canaanite military tactics and technology depended on whether their forces were from the north, with its increasingly advanced city-states, or from the less progressive south. In terms of the former, for much of the period considered, their armed forces would have been based on either the Sumerian or Akkadian model, depending on the period in question, more so later on. However, in the south, the forces were far less well organised. They coalesced only in times of tribal crisis or for raids on their neighbours, for example, Egypt to the south. The story of Sinuhe casts light on how these bands were led, with the chief being a leading warrior who had to prove his prowess in battle either himself or through a champion, also leading a personal retinue called a *henkhu*. Archaeological finds from hoards and tombs in southern Canaan indicate the warriors in these war bands were armed with javelins for missile weapons and flat and crescent-bladed axes, maces and daggers for close combat. A collection of copper plates from a hoard found at Kfar Monash has also been interpreted as some type of body armour.

Libya

The Libyan tribes that proved so troublesome to the ancient Egyptians lived in the vast desert stretching westwards from the Nile Valley. The first two referenced by the Egyptians are called the Tjehenu and the Tjemehu. The former are depicted as physically akin to the Egyptians and are thought to have moved westwards and away from their Nile Valley neighbours around the time of the unification by Narmer of Upper and Lower Egypt around 3,000 BC. However, the latter are depicted as being physically distinct and are thought to have had European origins. As time progressed, problems on the western borders of Egypt increased, and from the time of New Kingdom Egypt (1,549 BC to 1,077 BC) new Libyan tribes are referenced raiding into the Nile Valley. These included the Kehek, Libu (from where the name Libyan originates), Mahasun, Meshwesh and Seped. One of the reasons for this increase in border friction was climate change again, with the gradual desiccation of the Sahara from the west, driving the Libyan tribes eastwards. The levels of migration reached such levels that after the New Kingdom period some of the ruling dynasties in Lower Egypt became of Libyan origin.

The Libyans of the Early Dynastic and Old Kingdom Egyptian periods were nomadic herdsmen. They relied on a basic hunter-gatherer lifestyle, supplemented by the produce of goats and cattle. Shunning any built environment, they preferred to live in tents made from indigenously produced leather. However, over time, through contact with the various Egyptian dynasties in the Nile Valley, their political and economic sophistication increased. By the time of the later New Kingdom, this allowed them to form huge tribal coalitions under one leader to carry out massive assaults on the Nile Valley, the aim being to settle there.

Early Libyan warriors are depicted with a primitive array of weaponry, predominantly javelins but also with throwing sticks and bows. By the time of New Kingdom Egypt side arms are also referenced in the written record and shown in art, including copper swords. The latter were most likely supplied by allies including the so-called Sea Peoples (see Chapter 4). By this time their leaders are also depicted in two-horse, two-wheeled chariots very similar to those of the New Kingdom Egyptians.

Most Libyan warriors are depicted in art wearing very little, except a loincloth, though some have very bright cloaks and a few carry hide shields. The Libyan tribes often supplied auxiliary soldiers to the kings of Egypt.

CHAPTER 3

Genesis of Chariot Warfare

In Syria around 1,690 BC a revolution in military technology and tactics occurred, which came to dominate warfare for the rest of the period covered by this book. This was the adoption of the horse drawn chariot, and its use *en masse* as the main battle-winning component of Levantine armies from this time onwards. In this chapter, the origins of the chariot and its incorporation into the armies of the 2nd century millennium BC are considered in the context of three key cultures. These are the Hyksos Empire, the Hurrians and the Mitanni Empire, each considered in turn below.

The Hyksos Empire

As detailed in Chapter 2, the Hyksos were a Semite-speaking federation of Amorites and native Canaanites who conquered and then controlled Lower Egypt from 1,640 BC to 1,527 BC, so for most of the ancient Egyptian Second Intermediate Period and the very beginning of the New Kingdom period. Their name is a corruption of the Egyptian *Heka-Kheswet* meaning 'rulers of foreign lands'.

The travel south of the Hyksos wasn't the first migratory event into Egypt in the 2nd millennium BC. First, around 1,900 BC, Aamu nomads from the eastern desert settled in the eastern part of the Nile Delta. Then Canaanites began to appear here from the end of the Twelfth Dynasty around 1,800 BC. They established a cosmopolitan independent realm there of Canaanites, Aamu and native Egyptians. These first Canaanite settlers were driven south by increasing population pressure in Canaan following the arrival of the Amorites. The success of the Canaanite settlements in the Nile Delta proved an irresistible draw for others, and gradually their population increased at the expense of the Aamu and Egyptians. The migration then became a flood around 1,640 BC, when a full invasion of Lower Egypt took place. It is from this point that the Canaanites start being called Hyksos by the Egyptians. They consisted of numerous tribes under their own chiefs who swiftly overran Lower Egypt. These may have been suffering from famine and plague at the time, given the ease of the Hyksos conquest. The incomers established a new capital at the city of Avaris, which had previously been the capital of a *nome* in the Nile Delta. Here, they were ruled by a line of overall chiefs called the 'Great Hyksos'. The first, Salatis, actually managed to capture Memphis in Upper Egypt from the Egyptian king Dedumose. However, the Hyksos didn't stay long, choosing to consolidate their position in Lower Egypt. After a short period, Upper Egypt was left to its own devices as a vassal state of the Hyksos, though further south, the farthest reaches of Upper Egypt were lost to the nascent Nubian Kingdom of Kush.

Salatis's successor was called Yak-Baal, he in turn being succeeded by Khyan who styled himself 'Embracer of Regions'. Under his rule, the new regime expanded its trading contacts throughout the Levant, with the Hyksos state becoming a major regional power. Soon, the Great Hyksos began to use Egyptian names, the first to do so being called Apophis, with the nobility adopting native Egyptian culture including adherence to the Egyptian religious pantheon. Their principle God was Set, the local deity of Avaris.

The native Egyptian fight-back began under the Seventeenth Dynasty king Seqenenre II who ruled from 1,560 BC to 1,555 BC, at the very end of the Second Intermediate Period. Responding to an arrogant demand for fealty by Apophis, he campaigned in the north and lost his life in battle against the Hyksos, earning the epitaph 'The Brave'. However, even though the Hyksos captured

Memphis once more, the war continued. It proved a lengthy affair and only ended when the Theban king Ahmose defeated the last Hyksos king, Khamudy, in 1,532 BC, driving him and his court out of Upper Egypt and sacking Avaris. This was one of the earliest events of the Egyptian New Kingdom period. An Egyptian admiral, also called Ahmose, recorded this campaign. He says that when the Hyksos aristocracy realised they were defeated in Egypt, they fled back to Canaan, taking refuge in the wealthy city of Sharuhen (modern Tell el-'Ajjul, 6.5km south of Gaza). Ahmose the king besieged them here for three years before the settlement fell, it then also being sacked. The Hyksos were never to return to Egypt, and Ahmose's victory initiated the New Kingdom period of Egyptian history with the Eighteenth Dynasty. This was a far more militaristic time when ancient Egypt expanded to its greatest extent under the king Thutmose I, around 1,500 BC.

One intriguing manifestation of Hyksos rule in Upper Egypt is that, as foreigners, they opened Egypt up to external cultural influences. The most crucial, politically and economically, was the widespread use of bronze for weapons, scale armour, helmets and tools that occurred from this time. Egypt also began to adopt the composite bow, first used by the armies of Akkad, which as detailed in Chapter 2 became ubiquitous in New Kingdom armies. New fashions also arrived in Egypt in terms of dress and musical instruments, while new domestic animals and crops were also adopted from the north.

The Hyksos maintained a very large military establishment, with one later Ptolemaic Egyptian historian claiming the garrison at Avaris numbered an improbable 240,000 men. In terms of their equipment, it was long argued that it was the Hyksos who invented the chariot and introduced it to Egypt during their invasion, around 1,640 BC. However, this introduction is now known to have occurred at least 50 years before when we now know the first chariots are referenced in literature and epigraphy and found in the archaeological record in the region. Certainly, later in their rule of Lower Egypt, the Hyksos warlords made maximum use of the chariot and it is now thought they were introduced from Canaan after their rule in Egypt began. I argue below that it was the Hurrians who were the actual vector for this.

The chariots used by the later Hyksos were of a type ubiquitous throughout the Levant by the later 2nd millennium BC, called *merkhabet* in Canaanite. Drawn by two fast horses, their cabs featured a small D-shaped one-metre-wide fighting platform made of wood or interlaced leather thongs covered with a woollen or hide carpet. The 0.75-metre high sides, often open at their rearmost extremities, were made of a simple wooden lattice over which was stretched a fabric cover. These were often brightly coloured, with the finer examples having a coat of bronze scales to give some degree of protection. The well-sprung axle, enabling the chariots to operate across moderately rough terrain, was set well back and 1.5m wide. It featured two wheels, each with four spokes. As time progressed, this increased to six and even eight spokes. Meanwhile, the yoke-pole was 2.5m long. The horses themselves were small and could be protected by textile or scale trappers.

Each chariot featured two crewmen, the driver, who stood at the front of the cab, and a warrior. Both could be heavily armoured in scale mail, sometimes in a hauberk down to the ankles called a *sarium*. The main weapon was the composite bow, making the chariot a formidable missile platform. It came to dominate regional warfare, being used *en masse* to reduce an opponent's army through attrition, before the infantry engaged. Such was its success that it led to an arms race in the Levant, with each nation and city-state trying to outdo their opponents in terms of chariot numbers and quality. In that regard, it is this type of chariot that has become synonymous today with the armies of New Kingdom Egypt.

The infantry arm of Hyksos armies was well organised, reflecting the Amorite adoption of Akkadian military organisation. However, one change was the replacement of the Mesopotamian spear phalanx with swordsmen armed with sickle-swords or axes. Carrying shields, usually small, the preferred Hyksos tactic by this time was to charge headlong at the opposing army and engage in hand to hand combat as soon as the chariots had completed their work and retreated to the flanks.

The Hurrians

The Hurrians were a Bronze Age people from eastern Anatolia and northern Mesopotamia, who spoke a Hurro-Urartian language. Hurrian placenames are found from an early date in this region. They proved highly successful traders and farmers, and soon began to expand their cultural influence south and eastwards, eventually dominating an arc of fertile farmland from the Khabur river in modern Turkey (the largest perennial tributary of the Euphrates) to the Zagros mountains in modern Iran. They benefited in particular from the Hittite conquest of the northerly Amorite city-states in Syria covered in Chapter 6.

In the early stage of their expansion, the first known Hurrian kingdom was that which flourished from the 3rd millennium BC around the city of Urkesh (modern Tell Mozan) in the Taurus Mountains of north-eastern Syria. These were allies of the Akkadian Empire from the time of the king Naram-Sin, who ruled there from 2,254 BC to 2,218 BC. The Hurrians also migrated further south at this time, and by 1,725 BC they were to be found in parts of northern Syria, for example, in the city of Alalakh. From here, the mixed Amorite-Hurrian kingdom of Yamhad is recorded attacking the Hittite king Hattusilis I around 1,600 BC (see Chapter 6). Hurrian influence continued to spread southwards and eventually they replaced the Semitic-speaking Amorites as the dominant culture in Canaan. Across this region, now known as Syro-Canaanite, they came to rule a patchwork of prosperous and highly successful city-states. The most successful was the Kingdom of Mitanni, which is covered in a separate entry below. Others included the major coastal trading city of Ugarit in northern Syria, today on the outskirts of modern

Latakia. This presents an important Hurrian case study, given the finding of the Ugaritic texts there in 1928. These are a *corpus* of ancient cuneiform texts written on clay tablets baked by fire, when the city was destroyed in a raid by the Sea Peoples around 1,200 BC (see Chapter 4). Around 1,500, complete or fragmentary texts have been found to date, written between the 13th and 12th centuries BC. The most famous are approximately 50 epic poems, the three best known being the Tale of Aqhat, the Baal Cycle and the Legend of Keret. Other tablets either describe Ugaritic religious rituals, letters of correspondence or are legal and administrative texts.

The well-travelled Hurrians are important in this work because it was them who we now know introduced chariot warfare to the Levant. The Hurrian homeland was well placed to control trade between the Eurasian Steppe and the Levant, this being one of the reasons for their success. It was in the former that recent archaeological investigations have found the earliest known chariots. These were in *kurgan* burial mounds excavated in the Sintashta-Petrovka region at the southern end of the Ural Mountains, dated to between 2,100 and 1,800 BC. They have yielded the imprint of chariot wheels and other chariot-related grave goods, showing a clear lineage with those of the later Levant. Such technology would have travelled south along the trade routes to the Mediterranean, then being vectored south into Canaan, and later Egypt by the Hurrians. Some also believe that the scaled armour used to protect both horses and warriors referenced above, was also introduced into the Levant in this way, with the two technologies perhaps being linked.

The arrival of the chariot had a major societal impact in the Levant, with the introduction of a new class of chariot-mounted hereditary warrior nobility, called the *maryannu*. The name is first mentioned in the Amarna letters, a clay tablet administrative archive written between 1,360 BC and 1,332 BC by Egyptian scribes in this Upper Egyptian town, who were corresponding with the northerly Egyptian outposts in Canaan and Syria. The word comprises the singular Sanskrit *marya*, meaning 'young warrior', with a Hurrian suffix. Though service as *maryannu* differed in each individual state, such troops were usually hereditary landholders. There could also be more than one grade of service in the *maryannu*, and to confuse matters further, not all *maryannu* owned chariots, and not all charioteers were *maryannu*. Based on evidence from the Mitanni empire (see below), the term *maryannu* only referenced the chariot owner, with the bowman and chariot groom (the latter known as a *kizy* in Hurrian) being separately assigned crewmembers.

The Hurrians were known in the region as expert horsemen, over and above their introduction of the *maryannu* system of chariot warfare. A Hurrian manual on this subject, written by one Kikkuli, was found at Hattusa, written in Hittite cuneiform. It details that for both chariots and cavalry horses training began at one year old, though they didn't pull chariots until three years old. Those with the required skill would then be assigned to a chariot unit from the age of four, serving there until they were nine. Kikkuli's manual indicates that the horses were fed on barley and were regularly exercised by being driven or ridden a prescribed distance daily.

Ugarit provides a good example of the military organisation of the city-states of the Levant doing the period of Hurrian cultural domination. Here, again we have plentiful primary source material in the form of the Ugaritic texts. They show how cosmopolitan the region was, with military terms in Akkadian, Amorite, Egyptian and Hurrian appearing. Given its location as a coastal emporium, sea power was important to Ugarit and the state formally separated its land and marine arms into an army and navy.

An Ugaritic prince commanded the army. It featured a core of troops fully equipped by the state, including *maryannu* chariotry and foot soldiers, all called the *sabu nagib*. Each unit was commanded by an officer, called a *mur-u*, who was employed in this military role full-time. 'Officers of the Crown Prince' commanded guard units.

As with other Syro-Canaanite armies of the time, the *maryannu* were the main component of the Ugaritic army. Overall, they were commanded by an arkil *abrbakti* (Chief of Chariotry), with the elite chariotry being called the *ne'arim*. Given the location of Ugarit near to the Hittite Empire (see Chapter 6), some have speculated that the chariotry of Ugarit later evolved from the original light Syro-Canaanite model to a larger, and more, robust Hittite design. A wealthy state, Ugarit could certainly field a large number, perhaps up to 1,000. They frequently fought as allies of the Hittites.

The infantry component of Ugaritic armies was divided into three types. The first were the palace guards armed like other Hurrian-style foot troops with sickle swords (called a *khopesh* by this time) and axes. These would have formed the core of the infantry and wore leather corselets called *tiryana*. There was then a separate category of border troops who patrolled the countryside, armed with spears who were called *aweli imitti*, and finally a general call up of conscripted peasantry in times of trouble. The latter were called the *khepetj*. Skirmishing bowmen were called *medjergelem*. We know that the Ugaritic army campaigned far and wide in the region given that when the city was finally destroyed by the Sea Peoples (see Chapter 4), its land forces had been deployed to assist their Hittite neighbours in the north.

Meanwhile, the Ugaritic navy can be seen as a direct forerunner of that of the later seafaring Phoenicians from the same region. Its roles included supporting the army in the littoral zone along the coast and down river systems during campaigns, and also controlling the open ocean trade routes. In the latter regard, a key task was to deter pirate raiding by the likes of the Lukka from south-western Anatolia, the latter a main foe of the Hittites. The warships used by the Ugaritic navy were primitive monoreme galleys, these being the forerunners of those later used to such striking effect by Phoenicia.

The Kingdom of Mitanni

Mitanni was the leading Hurrian kingdom, existing from 1,500 BC to 1,250 BC. It has been called the first superpower in the Middle East. The kingdom's territory stretched from south-eastern Anatolia in the west, to the Zagros Mountains in the east. It came into being as a major power after the Hittites destroyed Amorite Babylon (see Chapter 6 for detail) during a weak period of Assyrian rule in northern Mesopotamia. From its capital city at Washshuganni (modern Tell al-Fakhariyeh), near the head of the Khabur River, the Mitanni rulers gradually extended their control over many of the cities formerly under Hittite and Assyrian control. These included Kizzuwatna in Anatolia, Carchemish and Aleppo in Syria, and Arrapha and Nuzi near Nineveh in the Assyrian heartland. The kingdom's rapid expansion was greatly aided by their preeminent use of the massed *maryannu* chariotry, for which they became famous across the region. Soon they had established a series of provinces, for example, the Hurrian Lands in eastern Anatolia, Hanigalbat in the Mitanni heartland of north-eastern Syria (and the name by which the kingdom was known in Assyrian), and Naharin in southern Syria (the name by which the kingdom was known as in Egypt). Mitanni's success as a trading empire spread far and wide across the region and it soon established a series of vassal states that provided an additional layer of border protection, this playing a major role in its longevity. These included Alalakh in Canaan, Arrapha in modern north-eastern Iraq, Nuzi in Mesopotamia and Ashur in Assyria.

Mitanni power reached its height under its early kings Paratarna and Shaustater, but soon its southerly expansion brought it into conflict with New Kingdom Egypt, itself then expanding under the empire-building Thutmose III. The subsequent war saw Egypt occupying much of southern Mitanni, though a counter offensive reclaimed this. A peace treaty followed after lengthy negotiations, with the Mitanni king Artatama I, marrying Gilu-Hepa, the daughter of Thutmose IV, to seal an alliance. The two nations then fought together under the Mitanni king Shuttarna I and New Kingdom Egyptian Amenhotep III against renewed aggression from the Hittite Empire in the north (again, see Chapter 6).

Mitanni power began a slow decline in the reign of the mid-period king Artashshumara. An anti-Egyptian faction at court, led by one

Ud-ki, assassinated him. The latter placed the dead king's brother, Tushratta, on the throne, but he then turned on his benefactor, had him executed and renewed peaceful relations with Egypt. However, the damage was already done, with the Mitanni court now riven by factions. The Hittites to the north seized on this and began a decade long process of encroachment along the northern borders of Mitanni. This proved highly successful and over time the provinces there fell one by one. The Assyrians to the east then followed suit, and by 1,250 BC, Mitanni territory had been reduced to the core province of Hanigalbat. This was finally reduced by the Middle Assyrian king Shalmaneser I, bringing the Kingdom of Mitanni to an end.

We have much detail of the organisation of the Mitanni military thanks to the numerous baked clay tablets found in the palace and other archives during archaeological investigations across the region. The warrior class, *maryannu* and otherwise, were broadly called *nakhushshu* and consisted of full-time professionals and a militia, the latter under obligation to serve the kingdom when called upon. This was known as *isharu* or *ilku*.

The *maryannu* system of warfare reached the pinnacle of its success under the Mitanni. Royal armies were built around a core of the king's bodyguard of elite charioteers, called *shepi sharri* (meaning 'the feet of the king'), 10 to protect him, and 10 the crown prince. Then, within the *nakhushshu*, the rest of the *maryannu* were called *alik seri* (veterans or campaigners). Each *maryannu* charioteer was then assigned a bowman and an *ahu* groom, as detailed above. In terms of equipment, a key innovation of the Mitanni was to drastically increase the number of chariot crew wearing full length scale armour.

Meanwhile, the infantry of the Mitanni kingdom was similar to those of the other Hurrian states, comprising charging infantry with sickle swords and axes and skirmishing bowmen. The former is depicted in epigraphy wearing leather armour and carrying round shields.

Maryannu chariots in action. (Simon Clarke)

The Dead Sea from the surrounding heights, a region much fought over in the period. (John Reid)

The usual deployment of Mitanni armies featured the infantry deployed in a deep formation in the centre and massed chariots on each flank. The latter sought to chase away the opposing chariot wings before enveloping the enemy foot troops. At that point, their own foot soldiers would then charge. The Mitanni often had a distinct advantage during the chariot engagement phase of a battle, given how well drilled they were. This was because combat between opposing *maryannu* chariot forces could be very confusing, the better drilled troops usually prevailing. Standards provided useful rallying points for the wheeling, shooting chariotry and were often targeted by their opponents. The capture of Mitanni standards in this way is recorded by the Assyrians.

CHAPTER 4

The Minoans, Mycenaeans and the Sea Peoples

We now focus on the early civilisations of Europe. Here, from around 2,700 BC, the Minoan culture flourished in Crete and on other Aegean islands. They were joined from 1,650 BC by the Mycenaean culture on the Greek mainland. The latter conquered the former around 1,450 BC, then suffering a major societal collapse themselves around 1,250 BC. This was the event that began the Greek Dark Ages. The downfall of the Mycenaeans caused widespread economic disruption across the eastern Mediterranean and may have been a causal factor in the emergence of the Sea Peoples at this time. These tribes of maritime raiders attacked the coastal regions of Anatolia, the Levant and Egypt, inflicting widespread damage. Where they were most successful, they often settled, a prime example being the Peleset, who, colonising Gaza, founded the Philistine Pentapolis there. It is from this that we get the name Palestine today. This period in European history is also famous for being the setting for Homer's semi-legendary Trojan War. All will be considered here.

The Minoans

The Minoan Empire was a thalassocracy, knitting together the numerous city-states of Crete and across the Aegean Sea. They did not speak an Indo-European language, which means they were not

Greek, but their actual origins are unknown. Evidence of Neolithic farming has been found in Crete as far back as the beginning the 3rd millennium BC. However, the first large cities didn't emerge here until around 2,000 BC, in association with an increase in centrally controlled agriculture. This saw the introduction of a highly successful system of intensive farming based on vines, olives and wheat. The first two grew well on the island's rocky mountain-sides, while the latter thrived on the fertile soils of the numerous river valleys. Sheep were also kept for their wool. Soon, the cities were producing a surplus. Much of this was shipped southeast to Egypt, north to the Aegean and Greece and northeast to Anatolia. The development of improved maritime technology enabled this trade to grow in the early 2nd millennium BC, and soon many of the Cretan cities were rich. Evidence of their far reach across the seas of the eastern Mediterranean can be found in Egyptian wall paintings created in a Minoan style, showing Cretans wearing their traditional kilts bearing gifts for the Egyptian king Thutmose III. The city-states expanded their power in their own localities, resulting in the creation of flourishing city-states. Later, fine quality Minoan pottery and copper and bronze metalwork were added to a growing list of goods they exported.

Minoan society was dominated by the huge palaces that formed the centre of each city. These are sometimes referred to as court buildings, given they were all built to a similar design around a large central courtyard. The leading cities by 1,800 BC included Phaistos, Mallia, Khania, Zakro and Knossos. It is from Minos, the mythical king of the latter, that the name Minoan is derived. Writing at the end of the 5th century BC, the Athenian historian Thucydides shows how important maritime prowess was for the Minoans (*The History of the Peloponnesian War*, 1.4).

> Minos is the first to whom tradition ascribes the possession of a navy. He made himself master of a great part of what is now termed the Hellenic sea; he conquered the Cyclades, and was the first coloniser of most of them, expelling the Carians and appointing his own sons to govern in

them. Lastly, it was he who, from a natural desire to protect his growing revenues, sought, as far as he was able, to clear the sea of pirates.

A cluster of subordinate cities and towns, these also featuring a central palace, surrounded each city-state. The palaces reveal much about Minoan culture. Each featured enormous storehouses for agricultural produce, including grain and oil. This indicates a high level of central-ised control, allowing the rulers to gather the produce from the city state populations as a tax, and then profiting from its export. The surplus also allowed the city-states to support a highly structured network of administrators, and an equally advanced military establishment. To facilitate this complex political system, the Minoans used an as yet undeciphered writing system known to us as Linear A. This, which was already in use by 2,600 BC, utilised a script based on conjoined lines that were used to make hundreds of different signs. The writing

Ceremonial Minoan double-header axe. (Wikimedia Commons)

system, mainly used for accounting, remained in use until 1,450 BC, when the Minoan Empire fell to the Mycenaeans.

Warfare was endemic between the various Minoan city-states, though interestingly most cities lacked a defensive wall circuit. This indicates that control of the sea was the most important aspect of Minoan conflict, with frescos at some sites showing amphibious assaults from monoreme galleys equipped with rams. At one time or another, one of the cities would rise to dominance, but around 1,700 BC the internecine warfare peaked with many of the palaces burnt to the ground. Most were soon rebuilt, though only Knossos regained anything like its former splendour. In short order, this city-state seized control of the whole island and reduced the other Cretan city-states to vassal status. In 1,626 BC, the palaces were again badly damaged, this time by the eruption of the volcano on the island of Santorini, which sent enormous ash clouds as far west as Cyprus. The tsunami this created would have devastated Minoan Crete. The palaces were again rebuilt, but finally fell out of use following the Mycenaean conquest.

Minoan armies were based around a chariot-mounted nobility and dense phalanxes of spearmen. The first chariots appear on Crete and across the Aegean from around 1,600 BC. This technology was introduced after contact with the coastal regions around the eastern Mediterranean. They were initially direct copies of the light chariots used by the various *maryannu* there, though in Crete they gradually became heavier with a larger fighting platform. To help the horses pull this more substantial design, an additional pole was added to the yoke pole, mounted horizontally with the first. It has been argued that this second pole actually went into the cab, dividing it into two fighting compartments.

The crew of these chariots differed substantially from the near-eastern counterparts. This was because instead of the fighting crewman being a bowman, here he was armed with a long thrusting spear. This could be used either like a lance, or, once the warrior had deployed on foot, indicating that the aristocratic chariot owner was this time the fighting crewman, rather than the driver. The earlier chariot designs are known as box-chariots in a Cretan context, while the heavier later ones are called dual-chariots. It has been argued that these later designs were more akin to battlefield taxis, rather than being used as a fighting platform.

Over time, the warrior in the chariot came to wear heavy armour. A fine example is provided by the Dendra panoply found at the village of the same name in the Argolis, Greece. This was the location of the royal cemetery of the city of Midea. The armour dates to the end of the 15th century BC and features a cuirass of hoops of overlapping bronze plates from the chest to the knees, with substantial three-piece bronze plates covering the shoulders and a large tubular turret neck protector sitting atop them. This ingenious corselet, called a *torake* (thorax), was assembled in two halves with the plates backed with leather and held together with a series of loosely fastened leather thongs. The individual plates were called *opawota*. The noble warriors equipped this way also wore bronze lower arm protectors called *qero* and bronze greaves, and a boar's tusk helmet with bronze cheek pieces. The chariot driver was less well protected. They are commonly shown wearing a padded quilt tunic.

Minoan spearmen are widely depicted across Crete and the Aegean, for example, in frescos from Santorini, and, later on a silver crater and decorated dagger from Mycenae. They carried a very long spear called an *eka-a*. This was held two-handed above the chest in a similar manner to the way pikemen carried their weapons in the European Renaissance. For protection, the spearmen are shown with boars tusk helmets and with very large body shields held in place by a leather strap, given both hands were being used to fight with the spear. Archaeologists call these tower shields. Given the size of this shield, few spearmen are depicted in any armour as, provided they kept their formation, there would be no need, with most simply wearing a loin cloth. They formed up in a shield wall, with archers and javelin men often shown skirmishing out from their ranks. Interestingly, many of the spearmen are depicted armed with elaborate bronze swords, indicating they were supplied from state-run armouries given the high cost of this elite weapon.

The Mycenaeans

Also called the Achaeans, the Mycenaeans were a Greek-speaking people who travelled to the Greek mainland from the northern Balkans around 2,000 BC. Here, they established a number of towns that, by 1,500 BC, had grown into large fortified cities with walls built from huge ashlars and featuring complex defended gateways. Major examples included Mycenae itself, Dendra, Pylos, Athens and Tiryns, with over 20 cities ultimately existing over the period of Mycenaean dominance in Greece. Through trade with Crete and the Aegean, the Mycenaeans adopted the Minoan Linear A script for use with their own Greek language. By 1,450 BC, this adaption had evolved into their own bespoke syllabic script called Linear B, the earliest written form of actual Greek. We are fortunate that this script, featuring around 200 signs, has been deciphered. At a number of sites, for example, Pylos, thousands of court records have been found on clay tablets baked when they were destroyed. These provide great insight into the daily workings of Mycenaean

The Lion Gate at Mycenae. (Wikimedia Commons)

Greek government. For example, the rulers were called *wa-na-ka*, an archaic form of the later Greek word *anax*, meaning 'master' or 'lord'. Further understanding of this warrior-centred society comes from the large number of richly furnished shaft graves excavated at their key settlements. These show great wealth, with the grave goods including gold, silver and electrum jewellery and tableware, gold face masks (including the famous 'Mask of Agamemnon' found at Mycenae) and bronze weapons and armour. From the 15th century BC, such burials evolved into even finer affairs, featuring vaulted *tholos*, beehive shaped tombs.

Mycenaean cities were ruled by kings supported by a warrior aristocracy, with the monarch often being the centre of cult worship. As with the Minoans, they lived in large palaces that formed the centre of urban life. Warfare between the cities over control of the region's agricultural produce and metallic raw materials occurred frequently, and from the beginning of the 15th century BC they began to expand their influence into the Aegean in search of new resources. By 1,450 BC they had conquered the Minoans.

As with their Cretan predecessors, the Mycenaeans enjoyed a thriving maritime trade across the eastern Mediterranean. A startling example of this has been found off Cape Uluburun, 8km away from the modern holiday resort of Kaş, in southwestern Turkey. Here, a Mycenaean wreck dating to 1,300 BC has been the subject of a meticulous investigation. Its hold was found to be carrying 10 tons of copper ingots and a ton of tin, the key ingredients to make bronze. The metal originated from Cyprus and the vessel was almost certainly on its way back to Greece when it founded, trying to round the headland.

The prosperous Mycenaean culture came to a shattering end some time after 1,250 BC, when all the key cities were burnt to the ground. A common explanation for this event has, until recently, been the arrival of the so-called Sea Peoples as seaborne raiders (see below). However, similar collapses are now known to have occurred elsewhere in the eastern Mediterranean at this time, for example, with the Hittite capital at Hattusa, 320km to the east of Ankara in modern Turkey, which was similarly destroyed. Archaeologists have now turned to climate change to provide an explanation for this region-wide catastrophic event, with pollen samples from cores taken from the bed of Lake Galilee, showing a sharp rise in plants that thrived in desert terrain occurring between 1,250 BC and 1,100 BC. This may have particularly affected Greece and Anatolia, with the Egyptian king Merneptah reporting that he had 'sent grain in ships to keep alive the Hatti (Hittites)'. This indicates a major famine.

The results in Greece itself were dramatic, with violent conflict between the cities breaking out over diminishing resources, as the fragile long-range maritime trading networks collapsed when the climate change event took hold. Soon, Mycenae and the other cities were deserted, with the palace culture and the Linear B script abandoned. A true dark age then descended over the Greek mainland, before the arrival of the Dorian Greeks, who from 1,100 BC, brought a new culture to the region, which saw the use of iron occurring for the first time.

A final note here in this historical narrative on the Mycenaeans concerns the Trojan Wars. These are detailed in the Greek poet Homer's *Iliad* and *Odyssey*, both most likely written in the late 8th century BC. The poems have an Ionic dialect, indicating they were written down among the Greek-speaking peoples of western Anatolia, the eastern Aegean Sea or the large island of Euboea just off the eastern Greek coast. They are amalgamations of many earlier oral stories and are often dated to the end of the Mycenaean period. The poems recall the abduction of Queen Helen of Sparta by Prince Paris of Troy, and the resulting Greek crusade to rescue her, led by Agamemnon, king of Mycenae.

Early Mycenaean armies were very similar to those of the Minoans, with the warrior nobility (called *eqeta*, or followers) riding to war in increasingly substantial two-wheeled two-horse chariots backed by dense phalanxes of spearmen. An early carved Mycenaean gem shows the fighting warrior on the back of a chariot still equipped with a long thrusting spear as with those of the

Mycenaean king charging into combat armed with a long spear.

Minoans. The chariots were still use *en masse*, with specific detail being provided on the numbers each state could afford coming from Linear B tablets at various key sites. For example, Mycenaean era Knossos could muster 400, while Pylos on the Greek mainland could field 82. The tablets also list the muster of individuals who would provide a whole chariot, or part of one.

One major change in early Mycenaean armies is noticeable, however, and that is with regard to the infantry. On frescos dating to this period, depictions of Mycenaean spearmen show the increasing use of a body-length figure of eight shield, as opposed to the earlier tower shield. This would have allowed the long spear to be used at waist level, rather than held two-handed at shoulder height, and also eased the use of the sword. It may indicate that the spearmen in Mycenaean armies had begun to utilise a more individualistic fighting style. This was certainly the case by the time of the Trojan Wars.

If the work of Homer is taken as fact, and this conflict is placed in the late Mycenaean period, then it is clear that later armies had evolved considerably from those of their Minoan and early Mycenaean forebears. Heroic charioteers still formed the elite core of the armies. However, as depicted on frescoes and other artwork, the fighting warrior in the cab had now replaced the long spear used as a lance with short spears and javelins. The *Iliad* also provides us with specific detail on how these chariots were actually utilised. This is on the context of the forces of Nestor of Gerenia, the Mycenaean king of Pylos. The poem details how the ageing though wise leader drew his chariots up *en masse* in front of his spear line. They were ordered not to get involved in a melee with the enemy, indicating they were now being used as hand-thrown missile platforms. Specific orders were given to the chariots not to break ranks, and one gets an impression of the chariots hurtling towards the enemy line, hurling a massed volley of javelins and then wheeling away. Eventually, the foot troops of each army would engage each other, with the chariotry then falling back to the protect the flanks. Many of the noble chariot warriors would no doubt dismount at this point to lead their foot warriors in combat. By the very end of the Mycenaean period, the change of chariot tactics evident here had begun to transform the actual design of the chariot to a lighter and less substantial model called the 'rail chariot'. This may have had completely open sides and was built specifically with speed in mind.

Meanwhile, the infantry of this late period changed even more than the chariot nobility in terms of their equipment and tactics. Gone once more now were the long spears, these again replaced by short spears and javelins. The more individual fighting style afforded by the figure of eight shield, clearly led to the adoption of looser formations, and by the end of the period these shields had themselves been replaced by simple round designs. This led to an increase in the use of body armour in the form of bronze or leather cuirasses and greaves. The boars tooth helmet remained ubiquitous. Interestingly, in the *Iliad* the literary device used to portray Nestor as very conservative is to describe his Pylian spearmen as still adopting the antique Minoan spear phalanx formation.

Both Homer and the archaeological record also show that missile troops formed a key, though subsidiary, component of Mycenaean armies. During the siege of Troy, both the Greeks and Trojans are described as using bow-armed specialist archers, either supporting the spear-armed troops or as skirmishers. Slingers were also used, though it was considered a lowly weapon. One particular depiction shows these various missile-armed troops in action. This is on the so-called 'Silver Siege Rhyton' found at Mycenae. This conical drinking vessel shows large numbers of naked archers and slingers reducing a group of cowering infantry, bearing large shields outside a walled city. One interpretation is that it shows inhabitants from the city fighting off sea-borne raiders. This was clearly a common occurrence among the cities of Mycenaean Greece.

We have great insight into the naval capabilities of the Mycenaean cities, both in the early and in the late period. For example, the epic Catalogue of Ships in Book 2 of the *Iliad* (2.494–759) lists the contingents of the Greek army that sailed to Troy. This not only includes the names of the leaders of each contingent, but also the number of ships required to transport their men to Troy. For example, Menelaus of Sparta required 50 vessels, the Cretans under their leader, Idomeneus, 80 and Pylos under Nestor 80. Given there were 29 contingents in all, this would have been a huge fleet. Late period Linear B tablets from Pylos detail how a fleet as large as theirs (in the Catalogue of Ships it was second only to that of Agamemnon from Mycenae) was manned. The tablets include a muster of 600

Sea Peoples' warriors ready for action. (Simon Clarke)

Levantine war galleys in action.

rowers needed for the part of the fleet based at Navarino Bay near the city, with the 20 ships there requiring 30 rowers each. Other ships needed larger crews, as in, for example, the frescoes from Thera (modern Santorini), showing vessels with a complement of 42.

Given this naval prowess, the Mycenaean cities took coastal defence very seriously. The Pylian tablets, again, provide a good example. This city had a long coastline to defend and so divided it up into 10 sectors. Each was allocated units of watchmen conscripted from local settlements, these in multiples of 10, with the maximum number being 110 for the longest sectors. The units were commanded by an officer with a second-in-command called a 'follower', who was equipped with a chariot. It was the latter's duty to travel inland at speed to report any menacing vessels approaching the coastline to much larger forces based there. As such, this can be seen as a sophisticated system of defence in-depth. It is likely that it was only set in place during the sailing season, from late Spring to early Autumn, given the date on the Pylian tablet is in the month of *Poroweto*, meaning 'sailing time'.

The Sea Peoples

As detailed above, the arrival of the maritime raiding Sea Peoples across the eastern Mediterranean was originally the causal event linked to the collapse of the Mycenaean and other regional cultures from 1,250 BC. However, this belief is no longer the case, and their appearance is currently linked to events following their downfall. In effect, the societal collapse of Mycenaean culture dislocated the regional economy to such an extent, that soon whole peoples were on the move from Greece, the Aegean and Anatolia, heading east and south for a new life in better climatic conditions.

The Sea Peoples are first recorded in 1,231 BC, arriving *en masse* in the eastern Mediterranean, where they began carrying out large-scale raids. They initially travelled in two waves, one advancing across northern and central Anatolia from the northwest, the other along the southern coast from the southwest. Egyptian records from the time give great detail about what happened next, saying:

> … the northerners were disturbed in their islands. All at once nations were moving and scattered by war. No land stood before their arms, from Hatti, Kode, Carchemish, Arzawa and Alashiya, they were wasted.

The Hittite Empire, already suffering from the destruction of their capital city Hattusa, in the event that caused the initial collapse of regional order, was hard hit by the new migratory waves and soon overwhelmed (see Chapter 6). Many of the rich coastal cities of Syria sent troops north to try to bolster their neighbour, the Hittites effectively acting as a bastion soaking up pressure from the advancing Sea Peoples. Stripped of their troops, this only left the cities open to attack, soon falling one by one to the Sea Peoples. Hurrian Ugarit provides one example. Here, a final desperate letter from the king asking for assistance from the then uncommitted neighbours is chilling. This was found baked onto clay tablets in the burnt ruins of the royal palace, saying:

> Thus speaks the king of Ugarit … Ships of the enemy have come, some of my towns have been burned and they have done wicked things in our country … seven enemy ships have appeared offshore and done evil things.

Other cities known to have fallen to the Sea Peoples in this instance include Ashkelon and Hazor.

Egyptian records show their own first experience of Sea People raiding was in association with an enormous attack by the Libyans. These had been forced east by a series of poor harvests related to the changing climate, their aim being a land grab in the fertile Nile Valley. Egyptian records say the Libyans were aided by five tribes of Sea Peoples, these called the Ekwesh, Teresh, Lukka, Sherden and

Sea Peoples' chariotry. (Simon Clarke)

Shekelesh. These tribes were part of the southern wave of migrants. The Egyptian king Merneptah beat off the attack, but only just.

Back in the north, further Egyptian records show that with the fall of the Hittite Empire and the frontier defences in Syria, the two Sea Peoples waves quickly moved on again, meeting up in Syria. Those that gathered there were called the Tjekker, Denyen, Weshwesh, Shekelesh and Peleset tribes. They initially settled in the land of the Amurru, which they decimated in short order. They then moved southwards and in 1,186 BC mounted an assault on Egypt from the northeast. This was finally halted at the Egyptian frontier itself, and only after a major national effort. Given their absence here, the Ekwesh, Teresh, Lukka and Sherden may have remained in Libya after participating in the failed attack there.

Egyptian records give us specific details about each individual tribe. These were:

- The Ekwesh, who may have been Achaeans from Greece. They are described as unusually fair-skinned.
- The Teresh, who originated in north-western Anatolia and were part of the northern migratory wave of Sea Peoples.

Sherden Sea Peoples on the charge. (Simon Clarke)

- The Lukka, heavily referenced in clay tablet correspondence between Ugarit and the eastern Mediterranean state of Alashiya, in Cyprus. They are first mentioned in the 14th century BC, when they are called renowned pirates and raiders. It seems likely they took advantage of the arrival of the Sea Peoples from further west to join in the mass raiding. One record from Hittite archives indicates they may not have had a choice, saying they themselves were the subject of early Sea Peoples raiding. Their homeland was in southern Anatolia and today gives us the name for this region, Lycia.

- The Sherden, also thought to have originated in eastern Anatolia. They too would have been caught up in the general raiding taking place west to east. Some Sherden later raided Egypt, after the period of massed migrations, and were recruited into the New Kingdom Egyptian army as royal guards. They are usually depicted with leather-faced shields studded with bronze discs, long bronze swords and horned helmets. The Sherden, clearly experienced seafarers, eventually moved to Cyprus and later settled in the island of Sardinia, to which they gave their name.

- The Shekelesh, also originating in Anatolia. Much later, at the beginning of the 1st millennium BC, they travelled to Sicily where they founded the indigenous Sikel culture, later encountered by the Greeks and Carthaginians. Here they also gave their name to their new home.

- The Tjekker, whose origins are unknown. They are later recorded settling in northern Canaan along the coast above the Peleset in Gaza. An Egyptian text called the *Report of Wenamun*, dating to the end of the New Kingdom period in the late 12th century BC, records they were still active as pirates. A specific raid is referenced against the iron age port site at Tel Dor on the Carmel coast of modern Israel. They are often depicted wearing crowned leather helmets.

- The Denyen, who came from the land of Danuna in south-western Anatolia. These were also caught up in the southerly migratory wave along with the Lukka and Sherden. In an event prior to this, the *Iliad* records an Anatolian tribe called the Danaeoi fighting on the side of the Greeks in the Trojan War, indicating they may originally have been Achaean settlers. After the Sea Peoples' invasions, some of the tribes returned to their homeland. We know this because in the 8th century BC a Hittite successor-state called Danuniyim is recorded in Anatolia. The Hebrew tribe called Dan has also been connected with the Denyen. As with the Tjekker, the Denyen are also depicted wearing crowned leather helmets.

- The Weshwesh, also called the Washwasha. These are one of the least recorded of the Sea Peoples. A link has been suggested with the Bronze Age city of Wilusiya in western Anatolia.
- The Peleset, one of the better-known Sea Peoples. They have been connected with the Pelasgians who are listed in the list of Trojan allies in the Trojan War. After the defeat of the Sea People attack on north-eastern Egypt, they remained in the region, settling in Gaza and, over time, setting up the Philistine kingdom (covered in Chapter 5). Personal names from here are linguistically linked with Luwian, an ancient language from western Anatolia. This seems to confirm the link with the Pelasgians. Meanwhile, the Hebrew kingdoms believed the Philistines originated from an island called Caphtor, which is associated with Crete in modern interpretations. If true, this shows that the routes taken by the Sea Peoples in their migrations were often complex, with the Peleset travelling to Crete from Anatolia, before then heading eastwards. As with the Tjekker and Denyen, they are usually depicted wearing crowned leather helmets.

The Sea Peoples' tribes are often depicted or described as arriving in a given theatre of operation by sea. They were led by kings and a warrior nobility who fought in Syro-Canaanitic style two-wheeled, two-horse chariots. These are often shown with three crewmen, comprising two warriors with javelins and shields and the driver. They were fewer in number than those in the armies of their regional opponents, reflecting the often-chaotic nature of the mass migrations. Two-wheeled wicker-work carts, pulled by four oxen, are also depicted in association with the Sea Peoples, but these probably illustrate migratory transports.

The majority of the troops in the Sea Peoples' armies were charging foot warriors armed with swords and shields, some wearing bronze or leather body armour. The swords used by a number of the tribes are shown as unusually long, and some have suggested that this innovation was behind the Sea Peoples' military success against all of their opponents, with the exception of the Egyptians.

Canaanite warrior dating to the period of the Sea Peoples' invasions of the Levant. (The Metropolitan Museum of Art, Gift of Sheldon and Barbara Breitbart, 1987)

CHAPTER 5

The Hebrew Kingdoms and the Philistines

The Hebrew kingdoms in the Bible lands were diminutive in scale compared to some of the enormous Empires that came and went across the region. However, their significance to world history is great. The period of independent monarchy from the time of Saul through to the final Babylonian conquest of Judah in the early 6th century BC, were significant formative years for the Jewish faith. The effects of this are still of great relevance today for many of the world's leading religions. Further, many of the books of the Old Testament in the Bible provide much detail, not only about the Hebrew kingdoms, but also about many of their neighbours, and through a long chronological period of time.

What is being considered here is the origins of the Hebrew kingdoms, through to the end of the period covered in the Book of Judges in the Bible. Then, the period known as the United Monarchy is covered, when the Israelites nominally had one king uniting them, followed by the period called the Divided Monarchy, when the two rival kingdoms of Israel and Judah were ruled by their own kings. Finally, in this chapter, the Philistines mentioned earlier are detailed, given their importance to the narrative of the Hebrew kingdoms, and, more broadly, across the region.

The Origins of the Hebrew Kingdoms

Hebrew tribes would have been among the Canaanites who settled in the eastern Nile Delta from around 1,800 BC, prior to the onset of the Hyksos kingdom there. They would have been drawn to the fertile land there, leading their flocks to graze among the tributaries. Some believe the move south was prompted by climate change, making their own lands in Canaan less viable for subsistence agriculture. A document from the Egyptian Tenth Dynasty (2,134 BC to 2,040 BC), describing Canaan and its peoples at that time, shows the land was marginal at the best of times:

> … bad is the country where he lives, inconvenient in respect of water, impracticable because of many trees, its roads are bad on account of the mountains. He does not settle in one place, for (lack of) food makes his legs take flight.

Those Hebrew tribes in the delta would have thrived under the cosmopolitan Hyksos dynasties that ruled Lower Egypt. It may be that the story of the Biblical Joseph's rise to power is a recording of an actual event during this period. However, with the defeat of the last Hyksos king Khamudy by Ahmose in 1,532 BC, they would have been exposed to New Kingdom Lower Egyptian predation. This peaked in the long reign of Ramesses II, who ruled from 1,279 BC to 1,212 BC. He decided to build a new fortified residence city in the eastern delta named after him, together with a satellite 'storage' city called Pithom. These needed vast quantities of mud bricks to be made, mortar to be mixed and heavy labour for the actual construction process. This required a huge amount of manpower, with the Hebrew tribes in the wrong place at the wrong time. It was at this time that the Egyptian 'taskmasters' detailed in the Bible, were appointed over them to aggressively oversee their forced labour.

However, it was in the context of another dramatic event that the Hebrew tribes under Moses managed to escape Egyptian dominance. This was the arrival of the Sea Peoples. As we have seen, the New Kingdom Egyptian king Merneptah (ruler from 1,212 BC and 1,202 BC) fought off two invasions of Egypt at this time, one by a combined Libyan and Sea People migration from the west, and one by the Sea Peoples alone from the northeast. Even though Egypt was successfully defended, it was clearly a time of great dislocation across the region and gave the Hebrew tribes their chance to break free and head back to Canaan.

The Bible records this as having been accomplished through a very circuitous route, around the Sinai Peninsula. This may have been to avoid the warlike Peleset now settling in Gaza. Eventually, the Hebrew tribes began their descent into Canaan in the early 12th century BC, under Joshua's leadership, with allegedly 40,000 warriors. It is his book in the Bible that narrates the story of the subsequent conquest of much of Canaan, telling of three campaigns in the centre, south and north of Canaan. These resulted in the complete destruction of many of the leading Canaanite cities, and soon much of the region was under Israelite rule. The key events are set out below.

Rough terrain in Canaan. (John Reid)

Early ones in the central campaign included the battle of Jericho, one of the first Canaanite cities the Israelites came across. This is the location of the famous siege where the walls of the city were rendered to the sound of trumpets carried by priests marching ahead of the Ark of the Covenant.

Next, the Israelites came across the city of Ai. Here Joshua used a clever stratagem, dividing his force into two. The smaller he deployed before the city. The inhabitants responded by sending their own much larger army to confront it. However, Joshua had deployed the bulk of his army out of site to the rear of the city, now undefended. They quickly occupied it, setting its buildings alight. When the native army tried to return, Joshua attacked it through the rear with his force.

Now the Israelites turned southwards to campaign there. Here, the inhabitants of Gibeon, a city to the north of Jerusalem, agreed a treaty with them. However, as a result, Adoni-Zedek, the king of Jerusalem, forged an anti-Israelite alliance with the fellow Canaanite kings of Hebron, Jarmuth, Lachish and Eglon. These gathered a huge army and put Gibeon under siege. The latter sent word to Joshua, who marched through the night to catch the Canaanites at first light still in camp. The Israelites attacked immediately, catching the Canaanitic army completely unprepared. This soon broke, with the Israelites carrying out a great slaughter as they pursued their fleeing opponents down the steep defile at Beth-Horon. The five Canaanite kings were later captured hiding in a cave, taken to Joshua, and executed.

The Israelites next subjugated the southern Canaanite cities in a very brutal campaign, an event set out in the Book of Joshua (10:40–42):

> So Joshua defeated the whole land, the hill country and the Negeb and the lowland and the slopes, and all their kings; he left none remaining, but utterly destroyed all that breathed, as the Lord God of Israel commanded. And Joshua defeated them from Kadesh-bar'nea to Gaza and all the country of Goshen, as far as Gibeon. And Joshua took all these kings and all their land at one time, because the Lord God of Israel fought for Israel.

Word soon reached the northern Canaanite cities of the Israelite devastation in the south. The biggest state there was Hazor, whose king, Jabin, set out to create his own alliance to challenge Joshua. With his alliance in place, Jabin gathered a huge army at the site of the water supply for the Canaanite city of Merom. This was a flat plain, suitable for him to deploy the hundreds of chariots in his force. Accounts of this battle are confused, but it seems Joshua was again able to use a surprise attack, this time on the Canaanite chariot and horse corals. The former, were burnt and the latter hamstrung, after which they then set about the Canaanite foot troops. Total victory followed, with 'not one left alive'. Hazor was then burnt to the ground and Jabin allegedly killed, bringing the northern campaign and Joshua's conquest of Canaan to an end.

On the campaigns of Joshua, I add a note of caution. We are clearly very reliant on the Book of Joshua here, and in many cases

Salt flats around the Dead Sea, more difficult campaigning terrain. (John Reid)

the archaeological record does not match the suggested chronology. For example, there is a debate among Biblical scholars about whether Jericho was as prominent a settlement at the time, as indicated in the Book of Joshua. This is because the archaeological record actually shows that the major 2nd millennium BC city may have been destroyed around 1,560 BC. Further, cities like Hazor had major wall circuits, and it seems unusual that the Israelites would have been able to reduce them as described. One factor in the Biblical account's favour here is that Canaan was the route through which the scourge of the Sea Peoples had taken in recent history on their way to attack north-eastern Egypt. In that context, perhaps, many of the various cities' defensive networks were in poor repair.

The Book of Judges was named after the chieftains and elders who led the various Hebrew tribes in the period from 1,200 BC and 1,050 BC, prior to the emergence of the United Monarchy under Saul. This was a time of great instability in Canaan because of the relative weakness of Egypt to the south. Previously, this great power had dominated the Levant, but after the Sea People offensives, it had retreated back to its core territories of the Lower and Upper Egypt. To protect their north-eastern border, they encouraged the Peleset to settle in Gaza, becoming a major regional power that evolved into the Philistine Pentapolis. Over time this came to dominate southern Canaan, growing into a major threat to the Israelites.

The first engagement of the period was in the north. This was the battle of Mount Tabor, fought for control of the fertile Jezreel Valley. Here, a resurgent Hazor had been harassing the Israelite tribes settled there with a large army under the command of a seasoned mercenary called Sisera. His force included 900 chariots. The judge Deborah responded by tasking the Hebrew general Barak with gathering an army to challenge the Hazorite force. He was initially reluctant, given the size of the opposing army, but agreed when Deborah said she would accompany him. The tribes of Machir, Benjamin, Ephraim and Issachar responded to the call to arms, and soon a force of 10,000 had gathered at Kadesh. The army then marched to Mount Tabor, the high ground that commanded the Jezreel Valley and Plain. Sisera responded by ordering the Hazorite force to counter the move, setting up camp at nearby Wadi Kishon. This was near flat land suitable for his chariots, giving the Hazorites an enormous advantage, as the Israelites had few, if any. However, a sudden downpour caused the River Kishon, which flowed down the south-eastern edge of the Jezreel Valley, to go into full flood. This soaked the flat ground, creating a quagmire that incapacitated the Hazorian chariots. Seeing this, Barak's Israelite army attacked down the slopes of Mount Tabor, their swift charge aided by the steep slopes. Such was its ferocity, the Hazorite army was quickly routed. The Israelites pursued aggressively as usual, slaughtering their faltering opponents. Sisera was one of the few to escape, asking for asylum with the neighbouring Kenite tribe. Though this was initially granted, he was later killed in his sleep when a tent peg was driven through his skull.

Midianite Arabs. (James Hamilton)

The final engagement from the Book of Judges considered here is Gideon's defeat of the Midianite Arabs. For a seven-year period the Hebrew tribes based in eastern Canaan had been suffering at the hands of their desert-living neighbours. This may indicate a climate issue once again, driving the Midianites into fertile Canaan more frequently. The lack of any central authority among the Hebrew tribes also added to the problem, with at first no coordinated response. The description in the Book of Judges shows the Israelites were facing a serious issue (6.34–35):

> … the hand of Mid'ian prevailed over Israel; and because of Med'ian the people of Israel made for themselves the dens which are in the mountains, and the caves and the strongholds. For whenever the Israelites put in seed the Mid'ianites and the Amel'ekites (their allies) and the people of the east would come up and attack them; they would encamp against them and destroy the produce of the land, as far as the neighbourhood of Gaza, and leave no sustenance in Israel, and no sheep or ox or ass. For they would come up with their cattle and their tents, coming like locusts for number; both they and their camels could not be counted; so that they wasted the land as they came in. And Israel was bought very low by Med'ian.

Eventually the Midianites set up a permanent encampment in the eastern Jezreel Valley, bringing their entire community with them, including wives and children. This provided the Israelites with an opportunity, for if they attacked here then the nomads would be forced to fight, given their numbers would restrict a swift withdrawal. The judge and prophet Gideon took charge, calling out a general levy of the Israelites. This produced a force of 32,000, which was much bigger than he needed, given his plan was a clandestine assault on the Midianite camp. He, therefore, whittled this down to 10,000, and then from these chose a picked group of 300 to carry out his plan.

Gideon then personally led a thorough reconnaissance of the Midianite camp, this revealing that they were in poor morale. All was now set. He divided his three hundred men into three groups, posting one to the north of the camp, one to the west and one to the south. This left open a route of retreat for the Midianites to the east. Here he had posted more troops to ambush any survivors.

Next he armed his warriors with concealed torches and horns. He then waited until the early hours of the morning, just after the Midianite camp guard had changed and the new sentries would still be half asleep.

The assault began with a speedy charge into the Midianite camp from the three directions. This achieved complete surprise, with the concealed torches used to set fire to the Midianite tents and horns to sow confusion. A massacre followed and soon the Midianites were in full flight. Those who escaped the ambush Gideon had set along the eastern exit route were pursued relentlessly, eventually across the River Jordan. Here Gideon eventually caught the Midianite kings, Zebah and Zalmunna. Both were swiftly executed, with the Midianite threat lifted once and for all.

Hebrew tribes in this period generally lacked the chariots used by their opponents. They made up for this by mastering the use of very aggressive surprise attacks. These would often take place at night or make clever use of terrain. Each of the 12 tribes had a distinguishing martial feature. For example, the Simeonites and Ephraimites are called the 'mighty men of valour', while the Gadites were fierce and swift and mountain terrain experts, and the Judeans known for their skill using a short spear and target shield. Meanwhile, the Isaachar were expert scouts, and the Benjamites trained to be ambidextrous and highly skilled with the bow and sling.

In this early period, when a muster was called it was usually by tribe. Each provided warriors in units decimal multiples of 1,000 (*a'laphim*), 100 (*me'eth*), 50 and 10. Each unit was commanded by an elected officer called an *is hayil*, with senior commanders called *sar*. All males of 20 years or older were eligible for the muster, which could create a very large force. Examples are the 40,000 Joshua was allegedly able to gather on first entering Canaan, and Gideon's 32,000. The Israelite system of organising their army was sophisticated enough for each leader to tailor their forces to the task at hand, for example, Gideon with his 300 chosen men when mounting his surprise attack on Midianite camp.

Very few images exist of early Hebrew warriors. Most likely they would have been armed using a combination of Canaanite and, increasingly, Philistine equipment. The better armed were equipped with a shield called a *magen*, a thrusting spear called a *romah*, and a bronze helmet called a *kobha*. The most common side arm was the ubiquitous sickle sword, though the vast majority of the militiamen would have simply been equipped with javelins and slings.

The United Monarchy

This title covers the reigns of Saul from 1,020 BC to 1,000 BC, David from 1,000 BC to 961 BC and Solomon from 961 BC to 931 BC. It was a period when the Israelites were nominally united under a single ruler. Yet, calling Saul the first king of the United Monarchy is actually somewhat of a misnomer, given in reality he was only the king of the northern tribes. Those in Judah to the south either opted, or were coerced into a coalition with him. Later, a virtual civil war broke out after he banished David from his court. The name United Monarchy remains problematic too. After Saul's death, when David was anointed the king of Judah, in the north one of Saul's sons called Eshbaal, was at first acknowledged king. Even after he was murdered and David established as the king of the whole kingdom, he still had to fight off two revolts. Further, in the reign of Solomon, which is usually portrayed as a tranquil period, we have the story of Jeroboam, who was encouraged to rebel against the king by a prophet and fled to Egypt, only to return after the king's death. This was one of the events that led to the formal separation of Israel in the north and Judah in the south, and the onset of the Divided Monarchy.

Saul is in many ways a tragic figure; a king struggling to govern among a people used to theocracy, a man profoundly suspicious of his former son-in-law, David, and a father dying surrounded by the bodies of his dead sons at the hands of the Philistines. He first came to prominence around 1,025 BC, when leading a band of warriors against the Philistines. In all probability, he was an

Israelite judge at this stage in his career. In a first bold move he attacked and seized the major Philistine fort at Gibeah (modern Tell el-Fūl in northern Jerusalem). He then followed this by ejecting the Philistine garrison at Michmash across the valley on the road to Jerusalem. Together, these controlled the route invading armies from northern Canaan took when heading south. The fame his twin actions generated, led to the inhabitants of Jabesh-Gilead appealing to him for assistance. Here, the Ammonite king Nahash had besieged the town. Saul called a general muster of the Israelite militia at a Hebrew tribal assembly presided over by the prophet Samuel. He then crossed the Jordan River with his new army and mounted the usual Israelite surprise attack. The Ammonites were swiftly routed, the siege lifted and, as a result, Saul was declared king of the northern tribes. The context was the need for a successful military leader who could unite as many of the Hebrew tribes as possible in the face of growing Philistine aggression in the south. To counter this, he adopted a policy of forward defence, designed to prevent any further encroachment by the Philistines and their allies into lands now settled by the Israelites.

His first offensive campaign was against the Amalekites, and from that point onwards he was always out campaigning against the enemies of his new state. He proved an effective military leader and brave soldier, in the process taking the first steps in modernising the Israelite army. This was necessary because of the threat posed by the Philistines and their powerful army.

Three explanations are given in the Book of Samuel as to how David came into Saul's service. The first, was due to his skill with a harp. The second, is due to his selection by the prophet Samuel. The final one and best-known, is of him being the slayer of the Philistine giant warrior Goliath, the army champion. This story is worth retelling given the insight it gives into the conflict between the Israelites and Palestinians.

Saul's army, at this time, was facing that of the Philistines in the Valley of Elah, a fertile region in southern Canaan. Both remained in camp, though twice a day for 40 days Goliath came out to challenge the Israelites to send a champion to fight him. They didn't, and for once Saul is portrayed as being afraid, given he didn't respond to the challenge personally. Instead, he offered a reward to anyone that would fight Goliath on his behalf. When his own warriors refused, the offer was taken up by the shepherd boy David who was there taking food to his brothers who were fighting for Saul. The king was reluctant to accept, but eventually did so, offering his armour to David. The boy declined, instead deciding to confront Goliath with his own sling and five stones specially chosen from a nearby river. After a verbal exchange David advanced to sling shot range, and launched a stone at the Philistine champion, hitting him squarely in the forehead. When the giant fell to the ground, David cut his head off. The Philistine army reportedly fled, with the Israelites pursuing aggressively as always, reportedly all the way to Gath and Ekron, the capitals of two of the five Philistine city-states (the other three were Gaza, Ashkelon and Ashdod, see below). Meanwhile, after his victory, David took the armour off his dead opponent as a trophy. He was then summoned to court by the king and began to make his name as one of Saul's professional soldiers.

At first the relationship between Saul and David was a good one, with the latter becoming friends with the king's eldest son Jonathan and then marrying his daughter Michal. Her bride price was apparently 100 Philistine foreskins. However, the king, already rejected by the prophet Samuel, became jealous of David's growing fame. David, alerted to the danger, fled the court. He eventually returned to his homeland of Judah where he began to gather a group of followers at the stronghold of Adullam, southwest of Jerusalem. Eventually discovered by Saul, he chose to flee with his by now 600 men to Philistine territory. These were organised into six *me'eth* of 100, forming his household warriors from this point. They settled in Gath under the auspices of Achish, the king there. From here they gave military service to the Philistines, with David being rewarded with his own fiefdom around the city of Ziklag, where he was recognised as a vassal. He was specifically tasked with protecting the Philistine border, with Judea to the north, and served Achish for a year and four months. During this time, he was always successful defeating any incursions from Canaan, and was particularly brutal in his retribution, but only against the non-Hebrew settlements there. These he actually protected, fostering his reputation in Judea with an eye to the future.

Back in the north, Saul was now trying to wrest control of the fertile Jezreel Valley from the Philistines. He decided to give battle on terrain suitable for the chariots of the Philistine and their Canaanite allies, hoping it would guarantee an engagement, despite the fact that his army still had few chariots. On the Philistine side, David took no part, given their other rulers were worried he would change sides. The engagement took place near Mount Gilboa. We have little detail of this battle, other than it was a major defeat for the Israelites. The army quickly broke, with Saul's sons Jonathan, Abinadab and Malchishua perishing. Saul himself, confronted by the Philistines and targeted by archers, chose to take his own life. His severed head was paraded around the capitals of all five Philistine city-states to celebrate their victory.

Both sides were now consolidated, with the Israelites abandoning their territory to the west of the Jordan River. Abner, Saul's uncle and the defeated Israelite army commander, then installed Eshbaal, one of Saul's surviving sons, as the new king. To confuse matters, back in the south, David was now crowned king of Judea, having carefully built up his support amongst the Hebrew tribes there. He moved his household from Ziklag to Hebron where he established his first capital. For seven years and six months he ruled there as a vassal of the Philistines, later also being crowned king in northern Israel, once Eshbaal had been killed by two tribal chiefs keen to ingratiate themselves with David.

Now in charge of the tribal militia, he next determined to move his capital to Jerusalem. This was a clever choice, given it was outside the specific territory of both the southern and northern portions of his kingdom. In the first instance though he had to capture the city, it being controlled by the Jebusites. David besieged the heavily walled settlement, and even though initial attempts to storm it failed, he hit upon a clever stratagem. This was to send a force of picked men through a water shaft into the city at night, while he diverted the attention of the defenders by attacking the walls with the rest of his army. The coup de main worked perfectly, with Jerusalem quickly falling to the Israelites. From that point onwards it became the 'City of David', a unique capital for his unique position. With the Ark of the Covenant installed there too, it also became the Hebrew religious centre.

We have no detailed accounts of David's campaigns or battles as he built his empire, though we can piece together a broad picture. In the first instance he suppressed the nearby Ammonites. Next he targeted the Philistines, his erstwhile overlords, who had become alarmed at his growing strength following the capture of Jerusalem. David fought two actions against them in the Valley of the Rephaim, a vale descending southwest from Jerusalem to the Valley of Elah. This was an important trade route from the Judean Hills to the coastal plane. He was victorious in both, pushing them deep back into their home territory. The Philistines then sued for peace, with David giving them the best settlement he would against any of his opponents. This was probably deliberate, designed not to provoke the ire of Egypt to the south who would have been aware of David's growing power. A result of the deal vassalage between the two switched over, with David now the lord of the Philistines, though the latter kept their day-to-day independence. Crucially, it gave David access to the key trade routes south through Gaza into Egypt. Additionally, the Philistine city-states became a key recruiting ground for mercenaries in David's increasingly professional army.

It was the cities of Transjordan that were to suffer the most from David's imperial expansion. Here, in the Aramaean Wars, David fought a series of vicious conflicts, including two set piece battles at Betrothal and Heram. At the latter, the Aramaeans allegedly lost

700 chariot teams and 40,000 men, including their army commander Shobach. After this, the Aramaeans withdrew from Transjordan, allowing David to expand northwards into Galilee, where he acquired a border with Phoenicia. This opened up control of the major trade routes to the north into northern Syria and Anatolia.

Next, David campaigned against the kingdoms of Moab and Edom. These were located on the Israelite southern border, conquering both. He then garrisoned the region to use it as a barrier against the raiding that was endemic from the nomads living in the Negev Desert.

At this point, David consolidated his position, having created a large kingdom with secure borders, profitable trade routes and a reformed army that could match any in the region in open battle. However, his next move caused outrage among many of the Hebrew tribes. This was to hand over of the surviving male relatives of Saul to their Gibeonite enemies. Though not unexpected, given it secured his own lineage, their fate shocked many when the Gibeonites dismembered them alive in an act of sacrifice.

Soon, tensions within his new state broke out into open rebellion. The first was led by his own son Absalom, whose conspiracy saw David displaced for several weeks. The motive was pure ambition, as he manipulated the growing tensions in the kingdom to have himself crowned king at Hebron. David fled to Jordan, while Absalom entered Jerusalem and took over the royal palace with its harem. However, he failed to pursue David and the latter was able to gather an army. David then moved to reclaim his throne, the final battle taking place at the Forest of Ephraim. He was quickly victorious, routing the rebels. Absalom fled, being killed with three javelins to the chest after his long hair was caught in the branches of a tree.

Next, the Benjamite Sheba started a rebellion among the northern tribes. David acted very quickly here, ordering his army in Judea north at speed. They caught Sheba and his rebels at the town of Abel Beth Maacah, which they put under siege. The inhabitants knew what to expect if they defied the king and, taking no chances, beheaded Sheba and threw his head over the wall. Thus, ended this rebellion, and the last major campaign of David's reign.

David was succeeded by his son Solomon in 970 BC. His reign was one of further consolidation, with Israel enjoying commercial prosperity thanks to extensive trade with Anatolia, Phoenicia, Egypt, Arabia and India. Solomon is most famous for the construction projects that monumentalised his thriving kingdom. The highest profile was the building of the first temple in Jerusalem to house the Ark of the Covenant. He was helped in this by his father David who, before his death, had already begun to gather the materials needed. Solomon himself oversaw the construction, hiring a famed architect called Hiram and making use of additional materials sent by another Hiram, the king of Tyre. The temple was built according to a Phoenician design. Solomon also built a new royal palace complex on a hilly promontory in central Jerusalem called the Ophel. This included buildings called the House of the Lebanon, the Porch of Pillars, the Hall of Justice and a royal residence for both himself and his wife. He also built a new wall circuit to defend his capital, and a new water supply system. Elsewhere in his kingdom, he built a new port city at Ezion-Geber, and a defended commercial depot at Palmyra to maximise the commercial potential of the caravan trains crossing the deserts from the east. He also rebuilt the cities of Megiddo, Gezer and Hazor, the latter probably still in a state of great disrepair after its destruction in the early Hebrew conquest of Canaan.

Solomon only had to deal with two military challenges during his reign, the rebellions of Hadad of Edom, and Rezon of Zobah. These were successfully curtailed. However, towards the end of his reign, his problems with Jeroboam from the Ephraim tribe would have far larger repercussions, as detailed below.

The military organisation of the Israelite army evolved greatly through the reigns of Saul, David and Solomon, to the extent that by the end of the latter's rule it could match any in the region. The armies of Saul were at first very similar to those of the early Israelite armies, based on a call out of the tribal militia. However, as his reign progressed, a formal organisation began to emerge, in effect creating a standing army for the first time. The core of this were the *ish bahur*, chosen men. These were professional soldiers, often mercenaries, attracted to serve under him given the opportunity for plunder as his kingdom grew. They numbered 3,000, being used in their first engagement to seize Gibeah from the Philistines, as detailed above. They were organised into three *a'laphim* of 1,000, enabling them to be deployed as required for each given situation. For example, at Gibeah, Saul divided the *ish bahur* into two groups, he himself commanding 2,000 *ish bahur*, and his son Jonathan 1,000.

This was the system inherited by David. He now styled his own personal household troops the *gibborim* (mighty men) and used these to create a new military organisation. In the first instance, he selected an elite group of officers from the *gibborim* called 'The 30'. The usual Israelite tribal levy militia was then formerly organised for the first time. This was into 12 divisions of 2,000 which in total gave David an army of 24,000 men. To create a standing army, he arranged for one of the divisions to be under arms each month, joined by the *gibborim*. This monthly gathering was commanded by one of 'The 30'. Thus, David now had a force on constant readiness to face any immediate threat. In times of conquest or crisis he could then choose how many additional divisions to call up. Additionally, David later created a royal bodyguard, over and above his own *gibborim*. This was made up of *Pelethites* (Philistines, the role model on which he created his new soldiery), and *Cherethites* (Cretans who were settled in the coastal region of southern Canaan).

The armies of David were still made up predominantly of infantry, armed and equipped in much the same way as those of the early Hebrew armies. However, David, for first time, had a few chariots, not enough to match those of his Philistine and Canaanite opponents, but enough for Solomon to later develop a full-size chariot corps. We get a sense of how many chariots David was able to operate by noting how many horses he kept for chariot use when he captured

1,000 in defeating Hadadezer of Zobah and his Damascan allies. Of these, 900 horses were turned over to the plough, with only 100 being kept for his embryonic chariot force. The chariots themselves were the same as those used by the other regional powers, with two horses covered in scale armour, two wheels with six spokes and an armoured archer and driver as crew.

By the time of Solomon, his wealthy state could afford a full chariot force that formed the centrepiece of his army. He was able to buy chariots at 6,000 shekels each from Egypt, and horses at 150 shekels, each from the Aramaean states of Syria, the Neo-Hittite states and Egypt. With these, he created a force of 1,400 vehicles and 12,000 chariot warriors, the latter called 'horsemen'. These included grooms and runners. The latter were usually armed as javelin men and worked to protect the chariots when in action. By the time of Solomon, these javelin men may have actually been mounted, with their horses then acting as spares for the chariot horses. This was part of a trend taking place across the whole region, eventually leading to the appearance of true cavalry.

To house his chariots Solomon distributed them across 12 'chariot' cities, each able to take up to 450 horses in their stables. This would have been enough for 150 chariots in three squadrons of 50, with two horses per chariot and one spare for the chariot runner. The 'chariot' cities were selected for their strategic importance, along key military routes and along the borders. They included Jerusalem as the capital, Balaath, Beth-horon, Tell-Kedah, Palmyra, Todamoor, Gezer, Megiddo and Hazor.

The Divided Monarchy

The United Monarchy peaked under Solomon but collapsed soon afterwards in acrimony. From that point on, it is called the Divided Monarchy. The split was caused by Jeroboam, the official in charge of the new walls being built in Jerusalem under Solomon. Encouraged by the prophet Ahijah, who said he would be a future king, Jeroboam conspired against the king but was caught. He promptly fled to Egypt where the king Shishak protected him until Solomon's death in 931 BC. He returned afterwards as part of a delegation to request a tax reduction from the new king, Solomon's son, Rehoboam. When the latter rejected this, 10 of the tribes threw off their allegiance to Rehoboam and made Jeroboam the king in the north. From this point, the territory here was officially called the kingdom Israel. Newly styled Jeroboam I, the king fortified and rebuilt Shechem as his new capital, where he constructed two state temples to compete with that of Solomon in Jerusalem. He installed golden calves in each. The towns of Bethel and Dan were then established as cult worship sites. Shechem proved a problematic choice of capital for the early kings of Israel, because it wasn't far enough north to project power into Transjordan. This had been under Hebrew control for many years. The capital was soon moved northwards to Tirzah, and later to Samaria.

Meanwhile, in the south, the remaining tribes stayed loyal to Rehoboam in Jerusalem, founding the new kingdom of Judah in the south. Sources for the early part of this period, including the books of Kings in the Bible, often tend to focus more on the northern kingdom than on its theologically more important southern counterpart, and that balance is reflected here.

The relationship between the two states was often fractious, even hostile, and during the 9th century BC Israel usually dominated Judea. As a counter, the latter often encouraged its ally Aram-Damascus to attack the former. Such disunity could be ill afforded by the Hebrew tribes as the key regional powers were once more reviving, particularly Egypt to the south, and Assyria to the north. For example, in 924 BC, the Egyptian king Shoshenq I invaded northwards, personally leading a campaign that passed through Philistine territory and then into Judea and Israel. As a result, many of the key regional cities were sacked. The two kingdoms were lucky to survive, then having to pay heavy tribute to Shoshenq. A turbulent period followed, with the Israelite king Baasha (ruler from 909 BC to 886 BC) exterminating Jeroboam's entire family. His son and successor, Elah, was in turn assassinated in 885 BC by Zimri, commander of half of the royal chariot corps. Zimri then took his own life when Omri, the commander of the Israelite army, besieged him in the by then capital Tirzah in response.

Under Omri, and later Ahab, Israel enjoyed a renaissance, and once more became a major regional power. Both kings played a key role in attempts to check the growing power of Shalmaneser III's Assyria. Omri was the sixth king of Israel, reigning through to 873 BC. He established Samaria as a new northern capital and stabilised Israel after its recent troubles. Contemporaries regarded this strategically placed site as impregnable. He then established peace agreements with Judah to the south and the Phoenician states to the north and campaigned in the east against the Moabites. There the latter's king Mesha conceded on an inscription 'Omri humbled Moab for many years', this making Omri the first king of Israel mentioned in a non-Biblical source. His later campaigning against the Assyrians also drew unlikely praise, with the mid-8th century BC Assyrian king Tiglath-Pileser III calling Israel '… the house of Omri' in his annals.

While the primary source references in the Bible regarding Omri are few and far between, a full six chapters are devoted to his son and successor Ahab in 1 Kings 17–22. This is because the timing coincides with the activities of the prophet Elijah, defender of the Hebrew God over the Canaanitic Baal, after Ahab had built a temple to the latter in Samaria. The Biblical account references the new king fighting three battles against Ben-Hadad, king of Aram-Damascus. The first was when the latter besieged Samaria, an Israelite surprise attack routing the Syrians. Next, a full-scale encounter between the two armies took place at Aphek on the south-east shore of the Sea of Galilee. Ahab was totally victorious, capturing Ben-Hadad whom he spared. However, the final battle at Ramoth-Gilead, in Jordan, was disastrous for the Israelites, with Ahab being killed. Interestingly, Assyrian annals record Ahab fighting in a coalition of 12 kings, including the king of Aram-Damascus against Shalmaneser III, after the latter campaigned south through northern Syria, capturing the cities of Aleppo and Hamath on the way. Here, we have specific detail of the size of the Israelite contingent, some 2,000 chariots and 10,000 foot soldiers. The former is considerably larger than the chariot corps available to Solomon, though in the event the Assyrians were victorious.

From this point onwards, both Israel and Judah found themselves part of the wider story of the later Assyrian, Egyptian and Babylonian Empires. Ahab's successor, Jehu, a former senior army officer who was highly regarded, given he had ridden his chariot near to Jehu's in battle, was forced to pay tribute to Assyria. A period of peace followed through much of the 8th century BC when Assyria went through a period of turmoil. However, the great Assyrian warrior king, Tiglath-Pileser III, then overran the entire Levant, reducing both Israel and Judah to vassal status. There are details here of the amount of tribute paid by Israel, with the king Manahem (who reigned from 747 BC to 742 BC) raising 1,000 talents of silver annually. To gather this amount, he imposed a tax of 50 *shekels* on his wealthy citizens. This proved so unpopular that his son and successor, Pekahiah, was later assassinated by a senior army officer. This was Pekah, who became the next king. He was a patriot who made a stand against subservience to Assyria, alongside his ally Aram-Damascus. They also tried to coerce Judea into supporting them but failed, the Judean king Ahaz instead appealing to Tiglath-Pileser III for help. This drew the inevitable attention of the Assyrian king, who was soon campaigning against them, destroying Aram-Damascus (the former's population was deported, and the latter sacked) and acquiring large parts of the territory of Israel. The Hebrew tribesmen who had lived in these areas, together with other Canaanites, were deported too. The annals of the Assyrian king show the brutality that could be expected to those who stood up to them:

> Israel ... all its inhabitants (and) their possessions I led to Assyria. They overthrew their king Pekah ... and I placed Hoshea ... as king over them. I received from them 10 talents of gold, 1,000 talents of silver as their tribute and bought them to Assyria.

With the backing of the Assyrian king it was Hoshea himself who overthrew Pekah, perhaps personally assassinating him. Like his forebear, he'd been a senior officer in the army, though its strength from this time is questionable, given the fact that the territory of Israel had now been reduced to the hills around Samaria, a difficult country for the Assyrians to campaign in.

At first, Hoshea kept his peace with the Assyrians, paying annual tribute to the new Assyrian king Shalmaneser V, after his predecessor died in 727 BC. However, he too succumbed to the temptation to rebel, perhaps encouraged by the Egyptian king So. He may also have thought the new king was less of a threat. He couldn't have been more wrong, and soon the wrath of Assyria was visited on Samaria itself. The Assyrians were expert engineers and found a means of circumvallating the supposedly impregnable fortress. A three-year siege followed, this a significant amount of time for a Biblical army to be kept in the field. Shalmaneser V meant to finish off this troublesome kingdom to his south, and this he did. However, shortly after Samaria fell to his warriors, he died before he could settle matters once and for all. The army then briefly returned to Assyria to resolve the succession. If the Israelites thought they had miraculously escaped their doom though, they were wrong, for at the first opportunity the new king Sargon II returned. He rounded up the entire remaining population of Israel that he could get his hands on, numbering 27,290 in total, and then deported them *en masse*. He also removed any remaining things of value in the diminished kingdom, including the precious chariot corps. The captives were sent to the farthest corners of the Assyrian world, including the 'land of the Medes', meaning modern Iran. This was as far from the Mediterranean world as one could be in the Neo-Assyrian Empire. Sargon II then rebuilt Samaria and peopled it with settlers from elsewhere in his vast empire. The kingdom of Israel was no more, and among the Hebrew tribes only the kingdom of Judah remained.

Here, the recently appointed king Hezekiah, in the first instance had to deal with a refugee crisis, given any people in the former territory of Israel who were able to escape the clutches of Assyria had fled south. Recent archaeology in Jerusalem indicates that this was indeed a real event, with an expansion of the population evident through a contemporary building programme newly revealed by archaeological excavation. The refugees included those tasked with maintaining the traditions and religion of their former kingdom, including scribes, priests and prophetic groups. Suddenly Jerusalem became the spiritual heir of Israel, sparking a reformation of sorts in Judah.

Hezekiah was newly empowered by these arrivals from the north. They would certainly have pressured him to assist in their return home. Soon, rebellion against Assyria was being discussed, and from around 715 BC, regional moves began to form a coalition of those states that had survived the previous Assyrian predation in the Levant, supported by Egypt. Word reached the empire in the north, and in 711 BC Sargon II moved first. He attacked and captured the coastal city of Ashdod, sacking it and deporting its entire population, including some refugees from Israel. This was enough to deter further opposition for the moment.

Sargon II died in 705 BC and was succeeded by his son Sennacherib. He inherited instability across his empire, choosing first to campaign in the east to quash opposition to Assyrian rule there. Then in 701 BC he turned his gaze south, hoping to nip in the bid any further problems in Judah. He invaded from the north and targeted the prosperous towns on the coastal plain there, sacking many, including Ashkelon and Joppa. An Egyptian army intervened to try to halt the devastation but was defeated at Eltekeh, with the Assyrians capturing all the Egyptian chariots. Sennacherib then headed inland, brutalising the region and capturing 46 walled settlements. Soon, 200,000 more captives were on their way back to Assyria. The conquest of one of these settlements, Lachish, is recorded on the gypsum wall panel reliefs from Nineveh displayed in the British Museum. These show the full narrative of the storming and sacking of the city. In particular, they show what those who opposed the Assyrian king could expect if captured, with the prisoners paraded before him as he sits on a throne, and then being executed and the bodies thrown into a pit.

Sennacherib's next target was Jerusalem itself, which he besieged. Hezekiah was expecting this and prepared the city well. The first Book of Chronicles says that he (32.5–6):

> ... set to work resolutely and built up all the wall that was broken down, and raised towers upon it, and outside it he built another wall ... he also made weapons and shields in abundance. And he set combat commanders over the people, and gathered them together to him in the square at the gate of the city and spoke encouragingly to them ...

The new exterior wall was built directly on top of demolished residential districts, some of the newly built houses for the Israelite refugees. Steps were also taken to prevent the besiegers using the local water supply. The most high-profile example of this was the redirection of the Gihon spring that supplied much of the water supply to Jerusalem. This normally filled a special pool in the Kidron Valley beneath the city. Hezekiah now ordered his engineers to dig a tunnel to reverse the flow of the spring, it then flowing into the newly created Siloam pool in the city itself. They also plugged the old fissure through which water from the Gihon spring had exited to prevent it being used as an access point by the Assyrians. In the event Hezekiah's preparations proved successful as Jerusalem held out and the Assyrians withdrew. The price for Judah was heavy though, with the Assyrian annals recording that:

> Hezekiah himself ... did send me (Sennacherib) ... to Nineveh ... 30 talents of gold, 800 talents of silver, precious stones, antimony, large cuts of red stone, couches with ivory, nimedu-chairs, ebony-wood, boxwood ... all kinds of valuable treasure, his daughters, concubines and female musicians.

The precious metals were stripped from Solomon's Temple and the royal palace precinct. The king also handed over much territory to the Assyrians in the coastal and Shephelah regions, which were then given to their loyal vassals. Hezekiah died three years later, his son Manasseh succeeding him, presiding over a lengthy period of total Assyrian domination of Judah. This included Manasseh himself being a captive of the Assyrians at the beginning of his reign. Later, he is recorded as one of 22 kings from the region who provided the Neo-Assyrian king Esarhaddon with building materials for public construction projects in Nineveh. Manasseh is later also recorded in a lengthy list of 'seashore' kings who assisted an Assyrian invasion of Egypt by Esarhaddon's son and successor Ashurbanipal. That Manasseh is listed among so many other kings in the region, shows how diminished Judah was by this time.

A brief renaissance was to follow. By the 630s Assyrian power entered a period of terminal decline and Judah briefly regained its independence under the king Josiah, who ruled from 640 BC to 609 BC. In a Judean military context, this period is best known for the battle of Megiddo in 609 BC when Josiah led his army to prevent an Egyptian force under the king Necho II, going to the aid of Assyria in their last stand against the Babylonians and Medes at the siege of Haran. The battle was very one-sided, with Josiah being killed in his chariot by an Egyptian arrow at the outset, as he oversaw the deployment of his army.

Judah now came under Egyptian overlordship. Having marched to the support of the Assyrians, Necho set up his regional head-quarters at Riblah (modern Ribleh on the border of Lebanon and Syria). Josiah was succeeded by his son Jehoahaz, who only lasted three years before being deposed by Necho and sent to Egypt, where he died. He in turn was succeeded by his own half-brother Eliakim, who Necho renamed Jehoiakim. However, a new change of overlord was just around the corner. The context was the defeat of the Egyptians at the crucial battle of Carchemish (modern Jerablus on the Euphrates), in 605 BC. Here, all the major regional powers fought a 'winner takes all' engagement, with the remnants of the former Neo-Assyrian Empire and Egyptians pitched against the armies of Babylon under Prince Nebuchadnezzar with his Mede, Persian and Scythian allies. The latter were victorious, with Assyria ceasing to exist once and for all, and Egypt retreating back to its home territories, never again to be a significant regional force.

Later, in 605 BC, the Babylonian prince became king as Nebuchadnezzar II, and Jehoiakim found himself in this brand-new sphere of imperial dominance. Nebuchadrezzar began his reign by campaigning in the Levant, capturing Ashkelon in 604 BC.

Around this time, Judah became a Babylonian vassal state. This allowed Nebuchadrezzar to lead his army to the border with Egypt in 602 BC, where an indecisive engagement took place. His lack of a notable victory emboldened Jehoiakim, who foolishly rebelled against the Babylonians. The result was an inevitable savage reprisal, with Nebuchadnezzar besieging Jerusalem in 597 BC. This was not the long-lasting affair of the earlier Assyrian siege, but a short and brutal business with the city capitulating on 16 March that year. The fate of Jehoiakim is uncertain, one report in the Bible saying he died during the siege, and another that he was taken in fetters to Babylon after the city fell. What is certain is that he was succeeded by his son Jehoiachin, who was also taken as a captive to Babylon along with treasure from the temple, other family members, key state officials, including military leaders and administrators, and all of the skilled craftsmen. In total, 17,000 were exiled, leaving only the poorest in society left in the city. Jehoiachin was to stay a captive in Babylon for 36 years, being released in 560 BC.

Now a shadow of its former size and influence, Judah was once more a Babylonian vassal. Nebuchadnezzar placed a brother of the earlier king Jehoahaz, called Mattaniah, on the throne, changing his name to Zedekiah. His 11-year reign is most notable for the final rebellion against Babylon, one that was to have disastrous consequences for Judea. Nebuchadnezzar once more descended on the kingdom, this time determined to finish it off once and for all. Soon, only the cities of Azekah, Lachish and Jerusalem were left to resist his might. These then fell one by one, Jerusalem succumbing last. Zedekiah tried to escape after the walls were breached but was captured. He was taken to Nebuchadnezzar's headquarters at Riblah, forced to watch his sons executed one by one, and then was finally blinded and taken as a prisoner to Babylon. Nebuchadnezzar totally destroyed the city and Solomon's Temple. The remaining population were exiled to Babylon, with any who could escape fleeing to Egypt. The kingdom of Judah was no more.

The armies of Israel and Judea were very similar to those of Solomon, though their chariotry would have been upgraded to the much heavier Assyrian and Babylonian four-horse battle-chariot models, detailed in Chapter 6, given the need to remain competitive with their opponents. Over time the 'horsemen' of the Unified Monarchy period evolved into full cavalry, though these remained junior to the elite chariot corps. They would most likely have carried out scouting and communications roles. Armies of the Divided Monarchy period also made much more use of allied troops and mercenaries than previously. These would have included Neo-Hittites, Aramaeans, Philistines, Egyptians, Phoenicians and Greeks. The latter were a particular innovation at the time, with many armies across the eastern Mediterranean recruiting troops from Ionia, and the Greek mainland equipped as early hoplites. These wore bronze helmets and cuirass, carrying the large round *aspis* body shield and fielded a long thrusting spear. Fighting in dense phalanxes of well-drilled spearmen, these warriors came to dominate regional warfare for the next 300 years.

The Philistine Pentapolis

For much of the period covered by the United Monarchy, the main threat to the Hebrew kingdom, and indeed later to Israel and Judah, was posed by the Philistines in Gaza. This lay to the south of Canaan.

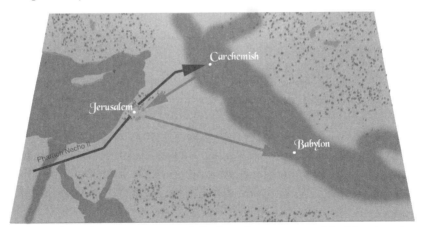

The Charchemish campaign in 605 BC where the remnants of the Neo-Assyrian Empire and their Egyptian allies ultimately lost a crucial battle against the combined forces of the Babylonians, Medes, Persians and Scythians. (Nigel Emson)

As previously mentioned, this kingdom had its roots in the Sea Peoples' invasion of Egypt when the Tjekker, Denyen, Weshwesh, Shekelesh and Peleset tribes tried to force their way into the Nile Delta from the north-east, during the New Kingdom period in 1,186 BC. Though repelled, they remained a threat. Ramesses III's response was to favour the Peleset, who were the most warlike of the tribes. He settled them as colonists in Gaza to act as a barrier to any further incursion from the north.

Here, they quickly prospered, with the five cities gifted to the Peleset by the Egyptians becoming the centre of thriving city-states. Three of these were strategically well placed along the Via Maris, the modern name for the ancient coastal trade route linking Anatolia and Syria with Egypt. The first of these, Ashkelon, had a fine harbour, while both Gaza and Ashdod were important emporia for regional trade. The latter was also a major fortress, as were both Gath and Ekron further inland. Ekron later also became an important centre for olive oil production. Together, the five were known as the Pentapolis. Later, a further important harbour was founded to the north of Philistia at Tell Qasile.

The five Philistine city-states were oligarchies ruled by a leader called a *Seren*, sometimes referred to as a prince. They ruled over both the Philistine and native populations in their areas of control, which were organised along feudal lines. Each *Seren* maintained a professional military class who held fiefdoms granted by the leader, for example that gifted to David by Achish of Gath. In return, they performed military duties as required by the *Seren*.

The foreign policy of the Pentapolis was determined by an annual council of the five *Seren* (together, the *Seranim*) called the *Sarney*. This came into its own after the death of Ramesses III, when Philistia embarked on a vigorous policy of commercial expansion, developing trade routes by both land and sea. Soon the Philistines were a thriving economic power in the region. The *Seranim* also appointed a military leader when the armed forces of all five city-states were deployed together. In that event, the gathering place for the combined force was at Aphek, to the east of the Jordan River. When this happened, it was usually in the context of protecting commercial interests rather than putting an army in the field for pure territorial gain. For example, the reason for most of the conflicts with the Israelites was over control of key trade routes and centres. In addition to the Via Maris, this included the retention of strategic centres in the Plain of Esdraelon, and at Succoth and Beth-Shean in the Jordan Valley. These allowed caravans of expensive goods from the east to reach Philistia by caravan.

In terms of their military organisation, the Philistines were early adopters of the chariot, based on the Syro-Canaanite model with two horses, an armoured archer and a driver in a small cab. They were renowned for their skill in its use, for example, at Mount Gilboa when chariot mounted archers shot down the fleeing Israelites. Over time the five city-states of Philistia built up significant chariot corps which, when combined, were the largest in the region. As with the Israelites and Judeans, the Philistines also later adopted cavalry for scouting and communications purposes, though they played little role on the battlefield.

The foot troops in Philistine armies were initially based on the traditional Sea Peoples' model of charging warriors armed with a variety of edged weapons, for example, the ubiquitous sickle-sword. At this time, they are often shown wearing crowned leather helmets. Later, however, through continuing contact with Egypt to the south, they adopted spear wall tactics using deep formations of armoured foot soldiers, armed with a short spear and shield. Goliath is described as such when fighting David. They also made extensive use of allies and mercenaries, with David and his *gibborim* again providing a good example.

The Philistines were well trained and used sophisticated tactics on the battlefield. For example, when the Israelites ejected them from Michmash at the end of the 2nd millennium BC they were formed into three columns and a rear-guard, the latter to cover their line of retreat. In this event and particular occasion, it was needed.

CHAPTER 6

The Hittite, Assyrian and Babylonian Empires

This final chapter considers the three civilisations under which military power peaked during the Biblical period. These were the mighty empires of the Hittites, Assyrians and Babylonians. Each came to dominate much of the modern Middle East, enduring peaks and troughs of influence before final dramatic collapses. The chapter closes with the conquest of Babylon in 539 BC by Cyrus the Great, the first Achaemenid Persian king. This was the event that marked the onset of the classical world.

The Hittites

The Hittites were an Anatolian people who established an empire from 1,600 BC, in northern and central Anatolia. This was centred on their capital later Hattusa, near modern Boğazkale in a loop of the Kızılırmak River, and the important city of Neša (modern Kültepe). It reached its height under the king Suppiluliumas I, in the mid-14th century BC, when its territory encompassed most of Anatolia, the northern Levant and upper Mesopotamia.

The Hittites are well referenced in both their own and Biblical sources. Given they frequently came into conflict with the Egyptian, Mitanni and Assyrian empires over territorial control of the Levant and the important trade routes there, many of their own records also reference the Hatti, as they were styled at the time. The Hittite Empire collapsed as part of the wider dislocation around the eastern Mediterranean from around 1,250 BC that also saw the destruction on the city-states of Mycenae. Its territory was then ravaged by the Sea Peoples, as they passed through Anatolia on their way to the Levant. After this, a number of Neo-Hittite city-states emerged, some of which survived until the mid-8th century BC, before finally succumbing to Neo-Assyrian expansion.

Hittite is the earliest recorded Indo-European language and is also known as Nesite and Neshite. Now long extinct, it is well attested in Hittite cuneiform records dating from as early as the 16th century BC. Many of these were recovered over decades of archaeological investigation at Hattusa, and include entire sets of royal archives recorded on clay tablets. From the later Bronze Age, it was gradually replaced as the day-to-day language in Hattusa and elsewhere in the Hittite Empire by another local language, Luwian. This remained the major language in the region through to the end of the Neo-Hittite period.

Little is known of the peoples who inhabited Anatolia prior to the arrival of the Hittites, though the rich tombs found at Alacahöyük, Dorak and in the Pontic region indicate the presence of wealthy settlements in the 3rd millennia BC. Anatolia was known in the ancient world for its mineral wealth, and by 2,300 BC Akkadian and Assyrian merchants began establishing trading colonies there. It is from the Assyrian traders that the Hittites later adopted cuneiform, sponsoring the development native city-states in central eastern Anatolia called *karums*. The key ones were Kanesh, Khurum, Wakhshushana and Dukhumid. The dominant local cultures, at this time, were the non-Indo-European-speaking Hattians in northern Anatolia (hence the later references to Hatti) and the previously discussed Hurrians in south-eastern Anatolia.

The Hittites themselves arrived in Anatolia at some stage before 2,000 BC, perhaps from the Pontic-Caspian steppe. Their societal organisation throughout all stages of their existence was distinctly feudal, with a system of obligation termed *iskhuil* or *ilkum*, permeating from the king downwards, often attached to gifted land ownership. Initially, the Hittites assimilated with the indigenous population, only gradually asserting their authority after the collapse of the Old Assyrian Empire, around 1,700 BC. Interestingly, there are no indigenous Hittite records of the initial migration of their forebears to the region. Their own origin story traced the roots of Hittite civilisation to King Pithana of Kussara, a bronze age state in central eastern Anatolia. Pithana conquered neighbouring Kanesh, the *karum* previously supported by the Assyrians, with his son Annitas establishing the city as his capital, after 1,750 BC. The Hittites themselves believed that their language originated here, and it was soon adopted across their growing territory. A later king, called Labarna I, who reigned from 1,600 BC, then extended Hittite control northwards to the Black Sea, and southwards to the Mediterranean, and around this time the capital city moved to Hattusa.

Old and Middle Hittite Kingdom

It is from the time of Labarna I's son Hattusilis I that we talk of the Old Hittite Kingdom. This lasted through to around 1,500 BC and was a time when the Hittites continually expanded their sphere of influence. The 'Telepinu Proclamation', an edict dating to the later reign of King Telepinu around 1,550 BC, says that:

> … (when) Hattusili I was the king, he and his sons, brothers, in-laws, family members, and troops were all united. Wherever he went on campaign he controlled the enemy territory with force. He destroyed their lands one after the other, took away their power, and made them the borders of the sea. However, when he returned from campaign, each of his sons went somewhere else to a country, and in his hand the great cities prospered. But, when later the princes' servants became corrupt, they began to destroy the properties, conspiring constantly against their masters, and began to shed their blood.

We can follow the campaigns of Hattusilis I from the written and archaeological record. He certainly advanced as far south as Aleppo, the capital of the Semitic Amorite kingdom of Yamhad in Syria, which he attacked but failed to capture. On his deathbed, he chose a grandson as his heir, perhaps reflecting the difficulties he faced with his 'princes', detailed in the 'Telepinu Proclamation'.

The new king was called Mursili I, becoming one of the greatest military leaders of the period. In the first instance, he succeeded where his grandfather had failed, capturing Aleppo in 1,595 BC. He next led a great raid 2,000km down the valley of the Euphrates River, skirting around Assyria and capturing Mari (modern Tell Hariri in Syria) and sacking Babylon, an event that caused shockwaves across the entire region. He ejected the ruling Amorite dynasties in both and installed his own vassals. One theory about why he embarked on such an epic campaign, is that he was seeking to bolster his national food reserves because the recent huge eruption of the volcano on Thera (modern Santorini in the Aegean Sea) had devastated harvests across Anatolia with its towering ash clouds. Another theory argues that, given the Kassites next took control of Babylon, Mursili had entered into an alliance with them and was campaigning to assist their own regional ambitions. Whatever the reason, it was to no avail, as upon his return the great conqueror was assassinated in a conspiracy led by his own brother-in-law who took the throne as Hantili I, and the latter's son-in-law who later became Zidanta I. The high cost in taxes to support the Euphrates adventure seems to have caused much unrest among the Hittite nobility, who supported Mursili's removal.

Mursili I's reign was the high point of the Old Hittite Kingdom. From the accession of Hantili I, matters became increasingly fractious among the ruling families, and through internal strife and civil war, much of the territory conquered by Mursili I was lost. Conflict on their southern borders with the Hurrians also proved a distraction for the Hittites, with the growing power of the Mitanni in Syria, detailed in Chapter 3, gradually usurping their influence there. The latter then encroached into the home territory of the Hittites themselves, establishing the kingdom of Kizzuwatna in modern Cilicia. The last Old Kingdom monarch of any note was the Telepinu, detailed above in the context of his proclamation. He fought campaigns in the south-east of Anatolia, where he won a few victories, actually allying himself with Kizzuwatna against the Mitanni. Telepinu also tried to secure the line of succession but failed, and, from this time until 1,430 BC and accession of the king Tudhaliya I, more instability followed. This period is known as the Middle Kingdom, when the Hittite northern borders were constantly assailed by the non-Indo European Kaska people of the Anatolian Black Sea coast. Because of this, the capital was moved from Hattusa to Sapinuwa, and then again to Samuha.

Hittite Empire

Matters improved for the Hittites from the reign of Tudhaliya, the ensuing era known as the New Kingdom or Hittite Empire period. He introduced a number of reforms that increased the power of the king, which stabilised the Hittite government. Crucially, he introduced a formal system of hereditary succession, which had been lacking in the past. He also took on key aspects of religious leadership in the kingdom that put him up to par with the kings of Egypt. From this point onwards, Hittite kings were known as 'My Sun' to their subjects, making annual pilgrimages to the Hittite holy cities, supervising the maintenance of religious sanctuaries and playing a leading role in religious festivals.

Under Tudhaliya the Hittite Empire began to expand southwards again towards Syria. In the first instance, he defeated Aleppo once more, in alliance with Kizzuwatna again, and then campaigned against the Hurrian Mitanni empire. The territory he captured increased the size of the Empire once more, and the Hittites prospered. However, despite the best efforts of Tudhaliya to shore up the stability of the kingship, a short period of instability followed his death, with four kings ruling for short periods. At this time, the former capital Hattusa itself was sacked, though it is unclear by whom.

A new strongman now emerged to take the throne, just in time to prevent another Hittite collapse. This was the great Suppiluliumas I, a new warrior king who reigned from 1,380 BC to 1,346 BC. He was the son of Tudhaliya II and his queen Daduhepa, quickly rising to become his father's chief advisor in court and his leading general. In the latter capacity, he successfully campaigned against the Azzi-Hayasa in the Armenian Highlands, and against the Kaskas. Tudhaliya II had actually been succeeded by Suppiluliumas' elder brother, Tudhaliya III. However, soon after his accession, Suppiluliumas led a coup and replaced his brother on the throne. He then set about a vigorous foreign policy that saw the Hittite Empire expand to its greatest extent, challenging all the great powers of the day.

His first campaign is known as the First Syrian War, lasting from 1,380 BC to 1,346 BC. Launching a lightning strike to the south, he soon conquered Aleppo, Alalakh, Tunip and Nukhasheshe, important city-states in northern Syria in the sphere of influence of the Mitanni empire. This triggered the Second Syrian War, when the latter counterattacked, only to be swiftly defeated by Suppiluliumas, who then launched a major strike into the Mitanni heartland. Soon, he had reached their capital at Washshuganni, which he sacked, then crossed the Euphrates south of Carchemish and marching south into territory controlled by the Egyptians, much of which he captured. He was emboldened here by the turmoil back in Egypt, given this was during the reigns of Akhenaten and Tutankhamun. After the latter's death, Egypt offered his widow to one of Suppiluliumas' sons in marriage. Eyeing a long-term alliance with the superpower to his south, the king agreed and sent his son Prince Zannanza to Egypt, where the wedding was due to take place. However, the Prince died on the way. Much speculation followed about the circumstances, with many in the Hittite court believing the boy had been assassinated. Suppiluliumas was furious and declared war. The Hurrian War quickly followed, where he captured Carchemish, defeated a New Kingdom Egyptian offensive, and then participated in the final defeat of the Mitanni, which was completed by the Assyrian king Shalmaneser I (see below).

New Kingdom Egyptian foot troops ready for battle. (Simon Clarke)

However, Suppiluliumas paid the ultimate price for his success, dying of the plague on his return to Hattusa. Contemporary reports indicate Egyptian prisoners captured in the Hurrian War had brought this back into Hittite territory. Suppiluliumas did leave the Empire in its strongest ever position though, with his sons placed as governors in the key cities of the Hittite Empire and with Babylon still under control of the allied Kassites.

After Suppiluliumas' death his eldest son, Arnuwanda II, ruled for a short time before himself succumbing to the plague. He was replaced by another of Suppiluliumas' sons, Mursili II. The new king's eastern territories were secure after the success of his father, so he chose to campaign in western Anatolia. Here, he attacked Arzawa and Millawanda, the latter a precursor to the later Greek city of Miletus in the south-west of modern Turkey. These were under the control of a people called the Ahhiyawa. One modern interpretation suggests the latter were in fact Achaean Greeks.

Mursili II reigned for 27 years, being replaced in turn by his son Muwatalli II, who ruled from 1,295 BC to 1,272 BC. He is best known as the Hittite king who led his forces against the resurgent Egyptian army of Ramesses II at the battle of Kadesh in 1,274 BC.

This took place on the Orontes River upstream of Lake Homs, on the modern border of the Lebanon and Syria.

The Battle of Kadesh

The battle of Kadesh is one of the best-recorded battles in pre-classical history, the earliest for which we have proper detail on the formations and tactics used, and the biggest chariot battle ever with

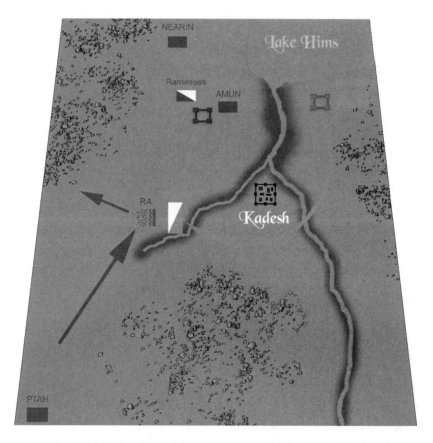

The Battle of Kadesh in 1,274 BC, one of the largest battles of the chariot era where the New Kingdom Egyptians faced off against the Hittites in a winner-takes-all engagement for dominance in the region. (Nigel Emson)

over 6,000 engaged. The major source of information regarding the battle is from the Egyptian perspective. This is in the form of two literary references known as the *Poem* and the *Bulletin*, these repeated numerous times in inscriptions at temples in Abydos, Karnak, Lzor, Abu Simbel and Ramesseum. There are also two references to the battle of Kadesh in papyri records called the *Papyrus Sallier III* and *Papyrus Raifet*. Finally, the battle is the main subject of a letter from Ramesses II to the later Hittite king Hattusili III, youngest son of Mursili II. This is in the form of a response to a complaint by the Hittite king about the accuracy of Ramesses' own depiction of the battle. Various Hittite references have also been found at Hattusa to the battle, though with less detail.

The context for the engagement can be inferred from the preeminent position the Hittite Empire now found itself in in the region. By this time, the Hittites were not only highly competent in the arts of war, but also in international diplomacy, with the sons and daughters

New Kingdom Egyptians on the attack. (Andy Unwin)

of its royalty and leading nobility married into the ruling families of its vassals and neighbours far and wide. The empire's diplomatic sophistication had reached a level whereby an ultimatum was always issued before military force was applied, while vassals in particular were tied into alliance by formal, complex treaties. These included a specific requirement to support the king when on campaign. As such, the Hittite Empire by this time posed an existential threat to the other two great super-powers of the age, Egypt and Assyria. It was the former that made the first direct challenge.

The battle of Kadesh was the climax of New Kingdom Egypt's expansionist foreign policy northwards into Canaan and Syria. This peaked under Ramesses II, with him targeting the kingdom of Amurru on the border of modern northern Lebanon and north-western Syria. At the time, this was either part of the Hittite Empire, or a Hittite vassal state. His objective was, therefore, to either capture it, or if it was a Hittite vassal, then to persuade them

New Kingdom Egyptian chariots. (Andy Unwin)

to change their loyalty to him. Either way, Amurru fought with the Egyptians at Kadesh, so in the first instance he was successful. Others have argued Ramesses was also there to scout out the ground for the future battle he knew was inevitable against the Hittites.

Muwatalli responded swiftly, especially when word reached him that Ramesses had future designs on Amurru's nearby neighbour, Kadesh. The Hittite king mustered what for the time was a huge army, including significant contingents from his vassals and allies. Ramesses later recorded the latter numbered 19 it total, including Rimisharrinaa who was the king of Aleppo. In total Muwatalli's force comprised up to 4,000 chariots and up to 40,000 foot troops.

We have far more detail about Ramesses' army given the number of Egyptian sources. He organised this into four divisions (based on the four New Kingdom army corps detailed in Chapter 2), these called Amun, P're, Ptah and Seth. Each approached Kadesh from a different direction and comprised up to 600 chariots and 5,000 foot troops. Ramesses positioned himself with the Amun division, which included his household troops, this taking the lead. His army also included Sherden mercenaries, the first time these later Sea Peoples are mentioned, and Canaanite mercenaries called *ne'arun* by the Egyptians. The latter were left near Amurru with orders to be ready to secure the nearby port of Sumur.

In the first instance, to approach Kadesh, Ramesses needed to cross the north-south flowing Orontes River at the Shabtuna ford. When he arrived there from the east, he redirected the *ne'arun* from their original place of deployment to cross the river first to form a screen for the rest of his force as he crossed. Then, one by one, the Egyptian columns deployed to cross.

Hittite agents pretending to be deserting Bedouin misled Ramesses at this point, convincing him that Muwatalli was still far away at Aleppo. This convinced the Egyptian king to lead his Amun column at speed over the river westwards towards Kadesh, where they began to make their camp for the night. Next in column to cross was the P're division, then Ptah and finally Seth. The latter was so far back it would take no part in the battle.

In reality, the Hittites were camped just the other side of Kadesh to the west, a fact Ramesses became aware of belatedly when some scouts were captured. This caused panic in the Egyptian camp, given P're had only just started crossing the river, with Ptah yet to start and Seth nowhere in sight. Ramesses sent his *vizier* back to hasten their arrival.

Muwatalli next pulled off a tactical masterstroke. Having isolated the Egyptian king and his division on the western side of the river from the rest of their army, he then sent 2,500 chariots in four divisions of his own to cross the Orontes eastwards, via another ford south of Kadesh. These circled the Egyptians on the east bank, and then attacked the P're division as it was crossing the river and the Ptah division, which was building its camp for the night. The Hittite chariots carried light troops as extra riders to bolster the size of the force, catching the Egyptians by total surprise. Soon, the Hittites had penetrated the Egyptian lines, destroying their chariotry and foot troops piecemeal. Many of the P're division fled west over the river, hoping for safety in the camp of the Amun division where they sought shelter. However, this only caused panic there, and soon the pursuing Hittites were hacking their way into the camp.

All seemed lost for Ramesses when salvation appeared from an unlikely source. This was the *ne'arun* who had earlier screened Amun division's river crossing. As the Hittite offensive stalled, with their troops intent on sacking Ramesses' camp, the Canaanites attacked the Hittites in the rear. This caused Muwatalli to deploy his reserve of 1,000 chariots to try to prevent the *ne'arun* cutting their way through to the besieged Ramesses. The reserve chariots failed, with the Canaanites joining the remnants of the Amun and P're divisions. Together, they now mounted six sustained attacks to try to break through the surrounding Hittites. At the last they succeeded, routing the Hittites, who fled. Some headed west to the Hittite camp, but many panicked and perished trying to cross the Orontes to the east.

As dusk neared, the Egyptians on the western side of the river now withdrew east under cover of darkness, forcing their way through the Hittite bodies in the river. On the eastern bank they made camp for the night. The following morning, sporadic fighting continued, though in reality both sides had fought themselves to standstill. Crucially, however, Muwatalli still held the field of battle, despite his final offensive on the Amun division camp being routed. He held off mounting a new offensive when he got word of the belated approach of the Egyptian Seth division. Ramesses used this force to block any further Hittite advance while he broke camp, then heading promptly back to Egypt. This left Muwatalli free to mop up any Egyptian and Canaanite stragglers, and as soon as the Egyptian army had left the region, he quickly seized back any territory Ramesses had occupied. The actual outcome of the battle has been much debated, given the clear spin of the Egyptian accounts. However, given Ramesses' speedy return to Egypt and Muwatalli remaining in possession of the battlefield, it was clearly a strategic victory for the Hittites. The one redeeming factor for the Egyptians was the resilience and professionalism of Amun division in holding off the assault of the Hittites until they were rescued by the *ne'arun*.

Muwatalli consolidated his position, then continued the campaign against Ramesses. He was determined to remove any future threat to his dominion from the south. Invading Syria, he captured the Egyptian province of Upi (modern Damascus), placing his brother Hattusili in post as the governor there. Outside of its own homelands, this left Egypt in control of only Canaan. Soon, the vassal states there began to threaten revolt against Egypt, no doubt encouraged by Muwatalli. Ramesses was, therefore, forced to campaign there, curtailing any plans to head back north and challenge Muwatalli once more. A later campaign did briefly capture land around Amurru and Kadesh, but this proved ephemeral and soon it was back in Hittite possession again. By now, both superpowers were worn out by decades of conflict along their borders and in 1,258 BC a peace treaty was signed with the Egyptians. This was inscribed on a silver tablet, a clay copy of which has been found in Hattusa. From this we know that one of the terms of the agreement was the marriage of a Hittite princess to Ramesses.

Muwatalli died in 1,272 BC, to be replaced by his son Mursili III. He was the Hittite ruler who returned the capital of the empire to Hattusa. By this time, the city covered an area of 1.8km, comprising both inner and outer areas. Both were surrounded by very substantial wall circuits, still visible today, erected earlier by Suppiluliumas I. The inner city, some 0.8km, comprised the royal residence (called the acropolis), the citadel, administrative buildings and temples. Mursili III himself died in 1,267 BC, after a brief civil war with his uncle, who then seized the throne as Hattusili III, the king who signed the final peace treaty with Ramesses.

One of the imperatives for this treaty from both a Hittite and Egyptian perspective was the growing power of Assyria. Already, this power to the east had begun serious encroachment on the Hittite border territories and vassal states there. Hattusili III's son, Tudhaliya IV, was the last king of the Hittite Empire strong enough to keep the Assyrians away from the Hittite heartland. He even managed to annex Cyprus, though he soon lost this to the Assyrians who also defeated him on land at the battle of Nihriva. The last king of the empire period was Suppiluliuma II, who himself was initially successful, winning a naval battle against a Cypriot city-state called Alashiya and a number of other engagements too. However, he soon lost more territory to the Assyrians, leaving the empire in a very weakened state. It is in this context that Hattusa was destroyed during the Bronze Age collapse after 1,250 BC, the empire as a whole succumbing to the subsequent predations of the Sea Peoples detailed in Chapter 4.

The Neo-Hittite States

Anatolia was devastated by the passage of the Sea Peoples travelling west to east for over a century. By the middle of the 12th century BC, however, a recovery of sorts had taken place, with the emergence of the Neo-Hittite States. Rather than being a single homogenous political entity, these were instead a widespread group of disparate confederations of city-states spread across the Anatolian and northern Syrian home territory of the former empire. We know them best through their conflicts with the later Assyrian and Neo-Assyrian Empires through to around 700 BC. One key point of difference is that by the time of the emergence of the Neo-Hittite States the use of Hittite cuneiform had disappeared, being replaced by a more primitive form of Hittite hieroglyphs yet to de deciphered. Luwian remained the main language spoken. The best-known Neo-Hittite States were:

- Tabal, in the Taurus Mountains in eastern Anatolia.
- Kammanu, to Tabal's northeast. Its capital was called Melid.
- Kummuhu, later to become the Hellenistic kingdom of Commagene.
- Carchemish, on the modern border between Turkey and Syria.
- Arpad, to the west of Carchemish.
- Til-Barsip, also to the west of Carchemish. This was a frontier territory with the Assyrians.
- Ya'diya, to the west of Arpad near the Mediterranean coast.
- Hattina in modern north-western Syria.
- Aleppo, also in modern north-western Syria.
- Hamath, also in modern north-western Syria.
- Adana, known to the Assyrians as Que, on the south-eastern coast of modern Turkey.
- Guzana, modern Tell Halaf in northern Syria. This was also a frontier territory with the Assyrians.

The establishment of the Neo-Hittite states also created the momentum through which a number of Aramaean states came into being in southern Syria on their borders. These included Aram-Damascus that, as detailed in Chapter 5, played such a key role in the story of Israel and Judah. Later Aramaean dynasties then usurped the Neo-Hittite rulers of Arpad, Til-Barsip and Guzana Ya'diya.

Those that remained found themselves increasingly under threat from the growing power of Assyria, and later Neo-Assyria to the east. Occasionally, coalitions of the Neo-Hittite states, sometimes joined by their Aramaean counterparts, came together to resist the aggression, but ultimately the whole region was swallowed into the vast empire of the Neo-Assyrian king Tiglath-Pileser III by 700 BC.

The Hittite Military Establishment

As with other armies of the period, the elite component of Hittite armies through all the various periods of its existence was its chariotry. During the Old and Middle Kingdoms these were very similar to the basic Syro-Canaanite types of Hurrian origin, not surprising given the latter were near neighbours. These were light designs with two horses and two wheels, with the axle set well back. However, one point of difference to the *maryannu* chariots in the south was the use of a third crewman, a shield bearer joining a spearman and driver. One of the crew could also be armed with a bow.

The chariot corps was supported by foot troops of various kinds. Such soldiers of the early period were also similar to their Canaanite counterparts, charging to contact using a variety of edged weapons. They were particularly known for the use of axes, some with very large axe-heads. Thin tapering spear points have also been found in archaeological excavations at Hittite sites, used on long thrusting spears. Troops armed in this way were deployed in loose formation rather than the spear armed phalanxes seen with the Sumerians, Akkadians, Minoans and Mycenaeans. As the Middle Kingdom progressed, the foot troops of the Hittite army became increasingly well organised, with regular standing army spearmen detailed in epigraphy and on cuneiform tablets.

We have much more detail on the armies of the Hittite Empire. The supreme commander of the Hittite armies of this period was the king himself who often led them personally on campaign and in battle. When he was engaged elsewhere, a senior prince would stand in. Divisions within the army were led by, once again, princes, and also the governors of conquered territories and rulers of vassal states. Groupings within the army were organised along decimal lines, in units of 10, 100 and 1,000. Specific units were termed *tuhuyeru*, and, at Kadesh, we have references to *tuhuyeru* of chariots, foot troops and so on.

A military aristocracy given land grants in return for service provided the chariotry of the Hittite Empire. Some compare these to the *maryannu* of Syria and Canaan, and certainly many of the latter would have been included in the multiple allied contingents often used in Hittite Empire armies. By this time most of the Hittite chariots were heavier than their earlier counterparts, perhaps reflecting contact with the Mycenaeans to the west. In part, particularly the axles, were set further forward, allowing a larger and more robust fighting platform to be used with better protection for the crew. These still numbered three men, a driver, spearman and shield bearer, by this time equipped with scale armour adopted from the Syro-Canaanite *maryannu*. By the time of Kadesh, the two horses pulling these chariots were also protected by scale armour, again as with those of the *maryannu*. One point to note here is that the large chariot corps of the armies of the Hittite Empire was by no means as uniform in terms of its equipment as those of their regional opponents. This reflected the cosmopolitan nature of Hittite society that embraced a variety of different cultures in Anatolia and Syria. Certainly, at Kadesh one can envisage a variety of different chariot types in Muwatalli's army, ranging from the newer and heavier Hittite types to the sleek chariots of their *maryannu* allies from Syria.

By the time of the Neo-Hittite States the chariot designs of Anatolia had evolved a stage further, this a response to the very heavy chariots used by the later Assyrians and Neo-Assyrians in the context of a Levantine arms race. Here we are fortunate to have many representations of Neo-Hittite chariots from this period, including detailed reliefs at Carchemish, Malatya, Sakjegozu, Tayanat, Tell-Halaf and Zinjirli. Other sources include the beautiful ivory plaques made in northern Syria that have been found in Nimrud. These would have arrived at the Assyrian city as tribute from a Neo-Hittite state. They all show a large fighting cab, the axle moved once more to the back on which were attached two large eight-spoked wheels. Four horses were now used, and the fighting crew increased to four. Such types are discussed in detail in the Assyrian entry below. Rather than being pure missile platforms, they were now designed for shock, being bulky enough to charge directly into enemy foot formations.

Another innovation of the Neo-Hittites was the use of full cavalry on the battlefield. Troops mounted in this way on equids had been a feature of Old and Middle Kingdom Hittite armies, and also those of the Empire period. However, their role then was usually for scouting and communications. However, following developments in Assyria once more, in the Neo-Hittite period, they acquired equal status. This was to the extent that at the battle of Karkar in 853 BC Assyrian records show that the armies of the Neo-Hittite Hamath and Aramaean Aram-Damascus had equal numbers of chariot and cavalry horses. One theory argues that by this time the cavalry operated alongside the chariots, perhaps providing a screen for the latter to allow them to position themselves where their shock value might be deployed to best effect. These Neo-Hittite cavalry are most often depicted armed with short spears, round shields with a central boss and a helmet, though some are also shown armed with bows.

In terms of the foot troops of the Hittite Empire and Neo-Hittite States, some were termed 'weapon-men' or 'tool-men'. It is thought this refers to the standing-army troops who were recruited from the artisan class who could afford their own military panoply. Their service was also connected with land ownership gifted by the king. These soldiers swore an oath as they entered the standing army to serve the king and state. They were then ritually cleansed before setting out on a given campaign, preparing them for the afterlife, should they not return. The cleansing process was particularly brutal, with the soldier marching between two posts, each of which had half of a human sacrifice tied to it. Their religious supposition was that evil couldn't pass between such a barrier.

These spearmen, called the 'fighting *tuhuyeru*' in Hittite records of the battle of Kadesh, now fought in close order formation using a short spear and shield. The latter could be oval, or a derivative with a half-disc removed on both the left- and right-hand sides to allow a spear to be deployed there. Such soldiers are usually shown armour-less except for a helmet, simply wearing a long kilt. For side arms they are shown with daggers and small axes. They were often brigaded together into large formations, for example, the two units of 18,000 and 19,000 foot troops recorded at Kadesh. Larger Hittite Empire and Neo-Hittite armies were bolstered with a levy of militia, deployed as above but more poorly equipped.

Hittite armies also made use of the traditional fighting skills of the various peoples who lived within their Anatolian borders and their neighbours. This included skilled skirmishers armed with bows, slings and javelins. It was also to vassals and neighbours that the Hittites looked for their naval power, given their extensive coastline for much of their existence. Examples at various times include fleets provided by Ugarit, Cypriot Alashiya and Lukka.

Old and Middle Kingdom Assyria

Assyria first rose to prominence in the 200 years after the fall of the Third Dynasty of Ur in 2,004 BC, when the Amorite cities in the north of its former territory began to coalesce into new kingdoms. The Assyrian state was largely Semitic-speaking and was centred on the Tigris River in upper Mesopotamia. Its homelands incorporated modern northern Iraq and north-eastern Syria, and later south-eastern Turkey and north-western Iran. The region took its name from the city of Assur, founded in 2,600 BC.

The first Assyrian king of note was Shamshi-Adad I, who reigned from 1,813 BC to 1,781 BC. A vigorous monarch, he gave form to the kingdom for the first time by building a state infrastructure around the cities of Nineveh, Assur and Arbil. Here the wealthy agricultural land, and access to the extractive raw materials to the north and west in the Zagros mountains and Anatolia, helped build a thriving economy that matched any in the region. Soon Shamshi-Adad I began to expand Assyria's influence, conquering the nearby city-state of Mari in modern eastern Syria. This era is known as the Old Assyrian Period, coming to an end about 1,700 BC, when Assyria first became a vassal of, and was then conquered by, the growing Hurrian Mitanni Empire, detailed in Chapter 3.

The Middle Assyrian period began with the reign of Ashur-uballit I, who reigned from 1,365 BC to 1,330 BC. He and the later Assyrian king Shalmaneser I, led the Assyrians in their assault on the failing Mitanni kingdom, the latter performing the *coup de grâce* that destroyed it. From that point, Assyrian power began to expand across the region again, with the capture of the Mitannian core territory of Hanigalbat, bringing Assyria hard-up against the territory of the Hittites for the first time. This prompted the latter to reach a peace agreement with Egypt, as detailed above, given the new threat to their east.

Assyrian war chariots in action. (James Hamilton)

The next great Assyrian campaigning king was Tukulti-Ninurta I, who reigned from 1,244 BC to 1,208 BC. He targeted the lower reaches of the Tigris and Euphrates valleys, destroying the Kassites then controlling Babylon. The kingdom then fought off a series of invasions from the northwest by a people contemporaneously called the Mushki, likely Phrygians. They were joined by Kaskas and Hurrians from the same region, the Assyrians eventually prevailing. They then counter-attacked under the great warrior king Tiglath-Pileser I (1,115 BC to 1,077 BC), who campaigned through northern Syria into Anatolia, savaging the Mushki homeland and then expanding the Middle Assyrian empire all the way to the Mediterranean coast. He then targeted the nomadic Aramaeans in eastern Syria, although he was less successful here, despite leading 28 campaigns. This failure had significant repercussions and by the time of his death the nomads had begun to settle within the southern and western borders of the Assyrian Empire. Successive Assyrian kings then failed to contain this threat and, soon, the emboldened Aramaeans began to encroach even deeper into the empire. The Assyrians were now forced back to their core territories around Nineveh and Assur, with the Aramaeans going on to overwhelm some of the Neo-Hittite city-states in Syria. The nomads then

Neo-Assyrians fight Midianite Arabs.

invaded Mesopotamia itself in 1,080 BC, and by 1,076 BC, the Middle Assyrian Empire had fallen.

The Neo-Assyrian Empire

Assyrian expansion began again under Adad-Nirari II, who became king from 911 BC, and from this time we begin to talk of the Neo-Assyrian Empire. Great kings of this period included Shalmaneser III, who fought the Israelite kings Omri and Ahab, Tiglath-Pileser III, who fought the Neo-Hittites and the Israelite king Pekah, and Sargon II, who fought the Neo-Hittite states and Urartians. However, their greatest ruler was undoubtedly Ashurbanipal, who came to power in 668 BC, and the narrative of this latest phase of Assyrian imperialism is best told through his dramatic story.

Ashurbanipal succeeded to the Neo-Assyrian throne in unusual circumstances. This was because his father, Esarhaddon, who had become king in 681 BC, passed over Ashurbanipal's elder brother Shamash-shum-ukin to make the younger sibling his heir. Why that

Neo-Assyrian four horse battle chariot. The main battle tank of its day.

was the case is not clear, but one cuneiform tablet found in Nineveh does detail that Ashurbanipal was the favourite grandson of the powerful queen mother, so perhaps some kind of court intrigue had a role to play. Interestingly, Esarhaddon himself had inherited the throne as a younger son, and in dramatic circumstances too. This was because when his own father, Sennacherib, named him the heir he was sent away to the western provinces for his own safety, a wise move given his elder brother then killed the king by stabbing him to death as he stood between two giant winged bulls in Nineveh while praying. Esarhaddon then watched from afar as the remaining princes in the capital fought out who should succeed as king, before smartly stepping in at the last minute to claim the throne for himself.

Lessons were learnt from the chaos surrounding the succession of Esarhaddon and, understanding of the necessities of maintaining a stable monarchy, a compromise was reached among the Assyrian aristocracy and military leadership to make sure there was no face lost by Ashurbanipal's elder brother, when the former finally became

A Neo-Assyrian army ready for battle. (Andy Unwin)

Neo-Assyrian mixed chariot and foot formation.

king. This was to make Shamash-shum-ukin the 'ruler' of Babylon, ostensibly as a joint monarch of the whole empire with Ashurbanipal, though in reality still owing fealty to his younger brother.

Once anointed crown prince Ashurbanipal entered the 'House of succession' for his princely training. Here, he received tuition on military skill, administration, mathematics, astronomy and scholarship. The former not only included strategy and tactics, but also martial skills to ensure he could hold his own on the field of battle. The abilities taught comprised chariot and horse riding, archery, the use of a sling and fencing. From this time, Ashurbanipal also shadowed his father to learn first-hand the duties of the king, later becoming Esarhaddon's spymaster. This gave him supreme knowledge of the empire's enemies and allies, information that would stand him in good stead later in life.

Ashurbanipal was the greatest of all Assyrian and Neo-Assyrian leaders of any period. His far-reaching empire featured a complex, integrated bureaucracy administering fully integrated provinces whose governors ensured the wealth of the empire made its way to the imperial treasury in Nineveh. This was all facilitated by the empire-wide system of state-maintained trunk roads and an integrated maritime trade network, both as sophisticated as anything later to feature in the Roman Empire.

Ashurbanipal claimed to be the 'King of the World', and there is no doubt that, in his day, he was the most powerful man alive. His first campaign, as he sought to expand the borders of his empire even further, was against Egypt. Here, he took over his father's campaign against the Kushite-Egyptian king Taharqa, whom he swiftly defeated in battle. The latter fled south to Memphis, where his nephew Tanutamun became king after his death in 664 BC. The new Egyptian ruler then set out with a huge army to liberate Lower Egypt from Assyrian rule. Here, Ashurbanipal had appointed Necho I as a vassal ruler. The Assyrian response to the Egyptian invasion was typically brutal, with Ashurbanipal marching south once more with his army including a number of allies from Canaan, these featuring Manasseh, the king of Judah, as detailed in Chapter 5. They savaged the Egyptians in battle again and then captured their capital at Memphis. This was systematically sacked. Tanutamun himself fled south the Kush, abandoning both Lower and Upper Egypt to the Assyrians. Countless Egyptian treasures, particularly from Memphis, were sent back to Nineveh to be paraded through the streets. The highlight was the melting down of the sacred metal Egyptian obelisks that had stood at the entrance of the temple gates in Thebes to help decorate Assyria's holiest shrines.

The next target of Ashurbanipal's ire was Elam to the northeast in modern Iran. This long-term enemy of Assyria invaded Babylon in 664 BC together with allies from the Aramean Gabmulu tribe, taking advantage of Ashurbanipal's focus further south in Egypt. The Elamite campaign stalled when their king, Urtak, died, but his fervently anti-Assyrian brother Teumann succeeded him, renewing the assault. Teumann's succession was actually a usurpation, given the rightful new king of Elam should have been one Ummanigash. The latter fled to Assyria where he sought the protection of Ashurbanipal. When Teumann demanded Ummanigash's extradition, the Assyrian king flatly refused, and once matters were resolved in Egypt, he then gathered a royal army, leading it personally to confront the Elamites in Babylon. Here, his brother Shamash-shum-ukin was struggling to contain the invading forces. A final meeting engagement took place at the battle of Ulai in 655 BC, where the Elamites were trapped against the Karkhere River near Susa and annihilated. Assyrian carved gypsum reliefs on the walls of the South-West Palace at Nineveh celebrate this victory, showing the river choked with Elamite bodies, many drowning as they attempted to flee the Assyrian pursuit. Other panels show the fate of Teumann and his elder son Tammaritu, both captured after the king's chariot overturned, and then brutally executed. Their heads were sent back to Nineveh.

Ashurbanipal wasn't finished with Elam and their allies however. First, he installed Ummanigash as his vassal there, dividing the kingdom up under governors also loyal to Assyria. He then turned his attention to the Aramean Gabmulu. These he defeated in battle, with their king Dunanu being captured alive. He and his family, and the leading Gabmulu nobility, were then led in chains back to Nineveh. Here, a particularly awful fate awaited them. Further gypsum reliefs from the Assyrian capital show Urartian envoys watching as their dreadful end unfolded. First, the heads of Teumann and Tammaritu were hung around the necks of Dunanu and his family. They were then paraded through the streets of Nineveh, being kicked and spat on. Dunanu was then splayed across a butcher's block and 'slaughtered like a lamb', his body parts then sent to the far corners of Assyria's vast empire. The rest of his family and the Gabmulian nobility had their tongues cut out for 'blaspheming against the true Gods', before being staked to the ground and flayed alive in an arena. On the relief panels the Urartian envoys continue to watch on, aghast. Such extreme brutality is clearly shocking to us today, but the Assyrians believed it was justified given what they viewed as the treasonous behaviour of the Elamites and Gabmulu. Ashurbanipal and the rulers of the Neo-Assyrian Empire believed they were the instruments of their Gods, bringing civilisation to those they viewed as the uncivilised. Thus, to Ashurbanipal, 'Assyrianising' all of the lands and territories of the multitude of peoples who lived within, and indeed without, his empire was a gift, allowing them to enter the lands of the Assyrian Gods. It is in this context that we should consider the even more terrible retribution visited on those who later dared to rebel against the king. This was in the context of recalcitrant Babylon and its allies.

This city, sitting astride the Euphrates River, was always a place of exponential importance in the ancient world, no matter whose sphere of influence it sat within. To the Assyrians it was a constant nuisance, never being able to manage it to fully integrate it as they had done with every other city within the empire. Babylon's sense of 'otherness' was exacerbated in the late Neo-Assyrian Empire period by how Ashurbanipal had come to power, with his elder brother Shamash-shum-ukin its 'ruler'. Ashurbanipal then caused more friction when Babylon suddenly found itself the focal point of his own personal flagship project, the one he intended to be his lasting legacy. This was the building of an enormous grand state library in Nineveh. Here he intended to collect all the written knowledge of Mesopotamia and the Levant under one roof. Building on the already impressive written collection of his father, he sent his court officials to scour every major centre of learning in the empire with orders to gather all the records found there, either as originals or copies. His plan was unprecedented in its ambition, and a key target was, of course, Babylon.

An understanding of the king himself helps us to comprehend his plan here. Ashurbanipal considered himself to be very much what would later be called a Renaissance prince. He was fluent in many of the languages of his sprawling empire and could read and write as well as any of his top scribes. Some believe that, as a younger son of the then king, he had actually been set for a career as a senior member of the Assyrian priesthood, leading to him being tutored in scholarship to a far greater extent than any of his other brothers. That set him uniquely apart from earlier Assyrian rulers, given the usual focus in their celebratory hagiographies on massacring their enemies and lion hunting.

Back in Babylon, even if Ashurbanipal only intended for his scribes to copy their precious cuneiform tablet collection rather than take them back *en masse* to Nineveh, the hackles of the ruling classes were raised. Matters finally came to a head in 652 BC when Shamash-shum-ukin then usurped against his younger brother, leading Babylon and a confederation of disenchanted vassals states and neighbours in a rebellion against Assyrian rule. Babylon's allies included the Elamites once more, the Mesopotamian Sealand state led by their king Nabu-bel-shumate, the kingdoms of the Guti and Amurru, and Chaldean and Arab nomads from the south. Ashurbanipal turned from scholar to warrior again, leading his army in a four-year campaign to stamp out the rebellion. Shamash-shum-ukin was killed either by an arrow or in a fire while fighting his brother. Soon afterwards, Babylon, which was under siege, surrendered in 648 BC. It got off lightly though, with a new governor installed, loyal to Ashurbanipal. Soon, their precious records were on their way to Nineveh.

Other members of the anti-Assyrian coalition were not so lucky, particularly Elam. It is here we see Assyrian brutalism at its most extreme. After breaking away from Assyrian vassalage to support Shamash-shum-ukin, they had then given sanctuary to the fleeing Sealand king Nabu-bel-shumate after their defeat. Ashurbanipal warned the new Elamite king Ummanaldash to hand him over or watch his country suffer an even worse fate than that which befell Elam in Teumann's day. When rebuffed, Ashurbanipal launched a lightning campaign deep into the Elamite heartland, destroying all before him and forcing Ummanaldash to flee to the Zagros Mountains. The Elamite capital was then flattened, its palaces and temples looted and burned to the ground. That, however, wasn't the end of the retribution. Given the royal family had fled, the nobility was rounded up and sent to Nineveh, once more in chains. Before leaving they were sent to the burial grounds where they were forced to gather the bones of their familial ancestors. Once in the Assyrian capital, they were then paraded in an arena, forced to grind the bones of their forebears to dust, and then finally executed in savage fashion. Seeing all hope lost, Nabu-bel-shumate committed suicide back in Elam, where Ummanaldash now returned to his wasted kingdom. Keen to restore any kind of peace with Ashurbanipal, he offered to surrender Nabu-bel-shumate's body to the Assyrian king. This he did, being taken into captivity himself for his troubles. He is last recorded yoked to Ashurbanipal's war chariot. One can only guess his ultimate fate. However, Nabu-bel-shumate was immortalised, given one of the wall panel reliefs from Ashurbanipal's palace in Nineveh shows his head decorating a tree in a palace garden. No more would Elam trouble Assyria.

Ashurbanipal spent the rest of his lengthy reign monumentalising his conquests with an extensive building programme, especially in Nineveh. This culminated with the construction of an exquisite royal pleasure garden, designed to rival anything in existence at the time. However, his death (or abdication, which is unclear) in 631 BC, marked the beginning of the end of the Neo-Assyrian empire. Things started to unravel in 626 BC, when a rebellious Chaldean general,

Neo-Assyrian Kallapani mounted infantry.

called Nabopolassar, seized the throne as part of an attempt to once free Babylon from Assyrian vassalage. A long civil war followed, with the Medes from modern central Iran appearing for the first time as new opponents of the Assyrians. Compared to some of the other cultures referenced here, the Medes may seem to us unremarkable. Yet, in their day, they were considered terrifying and unbeatable opponents, making great use of their fine bow-armed cavalry. Led by their king, Cyaxares, the Medes allied themselves with Nabopolassar and invaded from the north, sacking the Assyrian religious centre at Ashur, where they destroyed the temple of Assyria's supreme deity.

The Assyrians were caught completely off guard by the joint offensive, with Cyaxares and Nabopolassar now converging with their armies at Nineveh, which they besieged. This eventually fell in 612 BC, the Assyrian capital suffering the same fate it had visited on countless cities and peoples throughout the history of the Assyrian and Neo-Assyrian empires. It was thoroughly razed to the ground, with all the images of its once mighty rulers defaced and destroyed. The city's fall marked the end of the Neo-Assyrian empire, with Assyria never to rise once more.

The Assyrian Military Establishment

The military organisation of the armies of the Old Assyrian period was based on that of the neighbouring Mitanni, who eventually overwhelmed the empire. It was built on a system of feudal-style obligation to render military service to the king when called on, this called the *ilku*. The king himself often commanded his armies in person, though when that was not the case, a *turtanu* general would be appointed. The elite warriors were a *maryannu*-style chariot aristocracy riding in typical Syro-Canaanite two-horse chariots with two crew, one a scale-armoured bowman and the other the driver. The Assyria chariots of this period were noted for their skill in archery, though fewer in number than their Hurrian counterparts.

They were supported by a charging-to-contact body of infantry armed in the same manner as other such troops in the region with

Ashurbanipal makes an offering for victory.

sickle-swords and axes. The better equipped were variously called *sabum kibutum* and *ba'irum*, while the militia raised in times of crisis was called the *sabum qallatum*. They were supported by various light skirmishing troops armed with bows, slings and javelins. Armies of this period often also featured an allied component, for example, Amorite nomads.

By the Middle Assyrian period, the Assyrian army was much expanded and featured a full-time component, though was still visibly Hurri-Mitannian in nature. The most obvious change was a vastly increased chariot corps, with the fighting warrior in the cab now also armed with a spear. The best was known as the palace chariots and fought with the king, while the bulk of the chariotry were called the *Sha shepe*. Assyrian chariot archers in the Middle Assyrian period retained their prowess with the bow. They were supported by the first use of cavalry by the Assyrians, this in the form of *pethalle*, teams comprising an armoured mounted archer with a supporting lancer whose main function was to screen the bowman with his shield when the former was firing.

The foot troops of the Middle Assyrian period were much improved when compared to their Old Assyrian predecessors. The guard and better line troops were called *ashasharittu* (a derivative of the Assyrian word for prowess) or *huradu*, and were deployed in mixed formations featuring armoured spearmen supported in their rear ranks by bowmen. All were equipped with the typically Assyrian bronze conical helmets, with the spearmen also carrying a shield. For the latter, a variety of types were used, ranging from bronze embossed circular wooden types to more primitive designs made from woven read. Officers are often distinguished on decorative panel reliefs by carrying a mace. Later in the period, some *ashasharittu* could be transported on the battlefield by flat-bed carts called *kallapani*, pulled by two horses. These may have fulfilled a function similar to that of later dragoon mounted infantry.

The less well-equipped troops were known as *hupshu* or *sabe* and were armed in a similar way to the *ashasharittu*, though with few wore armour. Most were local militias called upon when needed. Once more, lightly armed skirmishers were also utilised, as were a wide variety of allied troops. All foot units were organised into *kisri* regiments based on a decimal system, with the basic unit of 10 warriors commanded by a *rab eshirte*.

Early armies of the Neo-Assyrian period were similar to those of the Middle Assyrian period. However, as part of the widespread reforms of Tiglath-Pileser III, the whole military establishment was overhauled. It is in this period, sometimes called Later Sargonid, that Assyrian military capability reached the height of its power. This king was originally a general called Pulu, who was placed on the throne following a revolt in the key Assyrian city of Nimrud. Taking the royal name Tiglath-Pileser III, he then set about his reforms. First, he re-ordered the far-flung empire into a series of provinces smaller than their predecessors. This was to diminish the chances of a governor leading a revolt similar to that which had placed him as king. The specific governors he chose were generals and administrators very loyal to him, many being family members. Those in the most important provinces were known as *bel-pihati* (noble lord), while those in lesser provinces were called *shaknu*.

Any border states that were deemed uneconomic for annexation into the empire, for example, in the deserts to the south, were still nominally bound to acknowledge the Assyrian king, with an official called a *qepu* (overseer) placed in charge of them. Meanwhile, neighbouring vassal states were newly bound by treaty to be loyal to the empire under the threat of destruction, should the alliance be breached. Next, a new courier system was created to bind the newly growing empire together using a new network of state-run trunk roads. Finally, Tiglath-Pileser III completely reformed the Assyrian military. To do this he created four different components within his armies. These were:

- The *qurubuti sha sheppi*, or household troops. These were the personal bodyguards of the king, queen and crown prince. They included elite chariotry, cavalry and infantry. Those of the latter tasked with the close protection of the royal family were called the *zuku shepe quradu* (heroes).
- The *kisir sharruti*, or 'the king's standing army'. This was a large force of professional troops deployed throughout the empire. They formed the backbone of any campaigning army, and comprised *narkabtu* chariots, *pithallu* cavalry and *suku* infantry. The latter were then subdivided into *nash azmaru* spearmen, *nash qasti* archers, slingers and shield bearers. Showing typical Assyrian pragmatism, the better elements of nations they had conquered were often recruited into the *kisir sharruti*. For example, Sargon II recruited 200 cavalry and 3,000 foot troops from Carchemish, 200 chariots and 600 cavalry from Hamath and 50 chariots from Israel. Large numbers of Elamite archers and Aramaean, Chaldean and Judean spearmen were also recruited.
- The *sab sharri*, or 'king's men'. These were semi-professionals auxiliaries under the *ilku* obligation to serve in the king's armies when called upon. They were often given land grants in return for being available when needed for military service.

Within the *sab sharri*, there was also a reserve soldier level for those over military service age called the *sha kutalli*.

- The *dikut-mati* levy militia. This was a general call up of all able-bodied men not already involved with the military. It was only called out in times of national emergency.

Given the size of the armies of the Neo-Assyrian period, Tiglath-Pileser III also introduced a new command structure for them. This set in place a new tier of general, beneath the king and his *turtanu*. These included those with new official titles such as *rab shaqe*, *abarakku*, *rab ekalli* and *rab-sha-rishi*. They commanded armies of varying size, ranging from huge ones in the range of 120,000 men led earlier by Shalmaneser III down to field armies of the size led by Sargon II, which included 150 chariots, 1,500 cavalry, 20,000 archers and 10,000 other foot troops.

The chariotry of the *qurubuti sha sheppi* and *kisir sharruti*, particularly in the Later Sargonid period, were much changed from their predecessors. Well represented on palace wall reliefs from across the empire, they were now much larger and designed not only as missile platforms but also as a shock weapon against enemy infantry formations. These huge chariots were drawn by four large horses protected with textile armour, featuring a large fighting cab and two large wheels with eight spokes. Four crewmen were now carried, all uniformly protected with a conical helmet now made of iron featuring ear protectors and wearing a lamellar corset of bronze scales. An archer is most frequently depicted, along with two shield bearers and the driver.

Armies of this period now also featured full cavalry, these having evolved from the *pethalle* teams of the Middle Assyrian period. Deployed in both the *qurubuti sha sheppi* and *kisir sharruti*, they wore a similar defensive panoply to the chariot crews and carried a spear and bow. Their horses are often depicted wearing protective leather coats. On occasion, the kings of the period actually fought with their cavalry rather than chariotry, for example, Sargon II, who led his own personal *qurubuti sha sheppi* cavalry unit of 1,000 into action. Meanwhile, the most exotic mounted troop type referenced for the Assyrians in this period was the dubious use of camels disguised as elephants by the Assyrian queen Semiramis against an Indian army.

The infantry of the Neo-Assyrian armies had also evolved from those of early armies and were now much better equipped. Foot troops of the *qurubuti sha sheppi* and *kisir sharruti* were again armoured in the same way as those riding the chariots, with the spearmen equipped with a variety of large body shields. The *zuku shepe quradu* are shown on palace guard duty and campaign carrying enormous round shields protecting them from foot to neck. These were made from a cone of bronze-coloured leather with a large central bronze boss and a bronze fringe. Other members of the *qurubuti sha sheppi* and *kisir sharruti* carried either a smaller variant of this, or a huge rectangular shield with a rounded top, also made of leather and fringed in bronze. The size of these shields indicates a desire to minimise casualties from missile fire, with the Elamites, for example, being famous for their skill with the bow. These spear formations were backed with integral missile troops, also armoured, with bows and slings.

Foot troops of the *sab sharri* were organised into the same style of formation as the *qurubuti sha sheppi* and *kisir sharruti* but were less well equipped. These replaced the bronze scale lamellar corset with a simple bronze pectoral to protect the chest, held in place with leather straps, and carry round shields made either of plank or wicker faced with leather.

The armies of the Neo-Assyrians also featured many specialist skirmishers armed with bow, sling and javelin, and a variety of allied warriors ranging from camel riding desert nomads to Kimmerian horse archers from the Pontic Steppe. In the very late Neo-Assyrian period, a specific regiment was actually raised of these latter troops, given their skill as mounted horse archers.

Finally, special mention should be given here of Assyria's expertise in siege warfare, particularly in the Neo-Assyrian period. Wall reliefs show a variety of techniques being used to render the walls of enemy cities in the various campaigns of the later kings. These included deployments of complex siege engines, mining and firing, the latter particular effective against the mud brick fortifications of the Levant. Siege engines included mobile or fixed siege towers equipped with massive iron shod rams or drills. Such towers were well protected with leather and wicker panels, and often featured a protected firing platform on top for archers and slingers.

The Babylonian Empire

The iconic city of Babylon has long held a special place for those studying the history of the Middle East from the earliest of times. It first comes to light as a military power in the Amorite Old Babylonian period, specifically with the sixth king of its first dynasty, Hammurabi who reigned from 1,792 BC to 1,750 BC. He campaigned successfully against Assyria and the city-states of Eshunna and Larsa, becoming Mesopotamia's most powerful ruler at the time. Hammurabi is best known for his law code that set out specific punishments for any crimes committed. He claimed to have received the code direct from Shamas, the Babylonian God of Justice, and was worshipped by many as a god in his own right during his lifetime.

The Old Babylon period and its first dynasty came to an end shortly after 1,600 BC, when the Kassites replaced the Amorites as the ruling class, with the support of the Hittite king Mursili I, as detailed above. These were a non-Indo-European-speaking people from the Zagros mountains. While little is known of their military activities, the Kassite's cultural influence set in place many of the institutions which were later to make Babylon such a shining light of civilisation in the region. For much of their period of control they were dominated by Assyria, and indeed it was the latter's king Tukulti-Ninurta I who destroyed their army and took control of the city, ending the Kassite period of control. Following this, local rulers reigned to little regional effect, the city then falling to the Elamites in 1,157 BC.

The next ruler of note was Nebuchadnezzar I, who was the fourth king of the fourth dynasty (and confusingly also the fourth king of the second dynasty of Isin, another regional city-state) and reigned from 1,125 BC to 1,104 BC. He led the Babylonian counterattack against Elam, being totally victorious and recovering the cultic idol of their main God Marduk. From that time through to the late 7th century BC, Babylon increasingly found itself the target of more Assyrian predation, particularly during the campaigns of Tukulti-Ninurta II, Shalmaneser III and Shamsi-Adad V. These penetrated deep into Babylon, extending Assyrian political control over the region even though the city itself wasn't conquered, retaining at least some form of autonomy. As with Assyria, Babylon next found itself the target of the unwelcome attention of nomadic Aramaeans in the later 11th century BC, with many settling within its borders. This led to instability in the region, which lasted 300 years, and in 728 BC the reforming Neo-Assyrian king Tiglath-Pileser III decided to intervene. He led an army into Babylon, forced the city to submit to his rule and made himself the king. From that point onwards, until the end of the 7th century BC, Babylon was ruled either by the reigning Assyrian king, or by an appointee loyal to Assyria. As detailed above, Babylon proved to be an ongoing problem for Assyria, often breaking out in open rebellion, this usually led by Chaldeans.

As the end of the century approached, the Neo-Assyrian empire began to fail, and another Chaldean stepped forward to seize control of the prized city on the Euphrates. This was the rebellious Assyrian general Nabopolassar, who set himself on the Babylonian throne. It was he, together with the Median king Cyaxares, who finally destroyed the once mighty Assyrians once and for all, as detailed above. The Babylonians were then ideally placed to step into the imperial void left by Assyria's demise, and this they did under Nabopolassar, and, particularly under his son Nebuchadnezzar

II, the nemesis of Judah. The latter's empire included all the lands conquered by the Neo-Assyrians, except Egypt, where he was rebuffed, this period of rule being called Neo-Babylonian. He is best known for his great building programme in Babylon, making it the greatest city of its day, including his famous hanging gardens which he built for his wife Amytis of Media, daughter or granddaughter of the Cyaxares.

The next three kings of Babylon were unremarkable and ruled an empire increasingly wracked with internal disorder. The Medes then turned on their former allies, with the Bible depicting them in a prophecy as the horrifying agents of God's wrath against the Babylonians (Isaiah, 13, 18):

> Behold, I am stirring up the Medes against them, who have no regard for silver and do not delight in gold. Their bows will slaughter the young men: they will have no mercy on the fruit of the womb: their eyes will not pity children. And Babylon, the glory of kingdoms, the splendour and pride of the Chaldeons, will be like Sodom and Gomorrah when God overthrew them. It will never be inhabited or dwelt in for all generations: no Arab will pitch his tent there, no shepherds will make their flocks lie down there. But wild beasts will lie down there, and its houses will be full of howling creatures.

However, it was a neighbouring Iranian tribe that was to finally destroy the Babylonian empire. These were the Achaemenid Persians of central Iran, former vassals of the Medes who turned on their masters and subjugated them before turning their attention to Mesopotamia and the Levant. Led by Cyrus the Great, they carried all before them and in 539 BC arrived at the gates in Babylon. Here, they captured Nabonidus, the usurping last king of Babylon, who was on his way back to the city after failing to engage them in battle. Kingless, the city fell without a fight, and so ended the Neo-Babylonian empire.

The Persians continued their aggressive policy of territorial expansion and by 500 BC they had conquered much of the Eurasian landmass from the western Mediterranean coast of Turkey, in the west to Afghanistan in the east. Contemporaries regarded them as just as fearsome as the Medes, with the Greek city-states believing them also unbeatable until the battles of Marathon in 490 BC, Salamis in 480 BC and Plataea in 479 BC. It is with the Persians that we finally get some insight into the enormous wealth that was at the heart of the various empires in the region covered by this book, ranging from Sargon the Great of Akkad all the way through to Ashurbanipal and Nebuchadnezzar II. We see this through the treasure captured by Alexander the Great when the Macedonian king, in turn, conquered the Achaemenid Persian Empire in the later 4th century BC. This was reported as 180,000 talents of silver, which would have weighed 4,600 tonnes. That is almost $4 billion in today's money and creates a direct link between the Old Testament and Hellenistic worlds. That is because it was fabulous wealth of this kind that funded the Hellenistic kingdoms that followed Alexander's death, and that later proved such an irresistible draw to the late Republican Roman warlords who led their campaigns of conquest in the east and established the later Roman Empire there.

The military establishment of the various stages of the Babylonian kingdom broadly tracked that of the Assyrians at the same chronological stage of its development. This only changed with the arrival of the Neo-Babylonian empire, when new troops types gave their armies a distinct difference to those of the Neo-Assyrians. While a chariot corps and cavalry still provided the elite troops of the army, armed in the same way as their Neo-Assyrians counterparts, the infantry were predominantly archers provided by Aramaeans and Chaldeans. Some of these were armed with pavises for protection and spears to give them some level of capability in close combat. Meanwhile, guard units equipped as the Neo-Assyrian *zuku shepe quradu* and small numbers of Greek mercenary hoplites provided the remaining line of battle troops.

Conclusion

As set out in the introduction, the chronological and geographic journey travelled in this book is vast. It has taken in some of the largest empires and greatest kings, queens and conquerors ever in existence. Such is its extent, that it is useful here in the conclusion to set out a few specific themes to consider in order to give my final thoughts accessible form. These themes are the military capabilities of the various civilisations and cultures covered, the importance of literacy, and their cultural legacies.

In terms of military capability, a wide range of examples are covered in the book. Interestingly, some of the earlier civilisations are actually among the most complex. That is certainly the case with the later armies of Sumer and Akkad. We see in their organisation the first complex battlefield technologies, with their battle cars, and also the first complex tactics with their spear-armed phalanxes. The fact that both developed further from their earliest iterations to later variants, also shows an innate ability to evolve, based on their experiences on campaign and in battle. Given its far reaching empire, the armies of the Akkadian empire also showed the aptitude to tailor a military force for a given campaign, with, for example, more auxiliary troops and fewer battle cars and spearmen used in campaigns such as the one against Dilmun in modern Bahrain.

Next, it comes as somewhat of a surprise to find the armies of Pre-Dynastic and Early Dynastic Egypt somewhat less advanced than their Mesopotamian contemporaries. However, this simply reflects the opponents they faced in Nubia, Canaan and Libya, or in the civil wars between Upper and lower Egypt. Certainly, later exposure to the rapidly developing cultures of northern Canaan, Anatolia and the region of modern Syria enabled them to rapidly catch up, such that by the New Kingdom period the Egyptian military establishment was one of the most capable on the planet.

In that regard, the defining image of this book is of course the chariot, whose origins are discussed in detail in the Chapter 3. Here, the Hurrians are identified as the vector through which the two-wheeled, two-horse chariot equipped with a driver and a bowman or spearman arrived in the region from its central Asian steppe roots. Soon the entire geography covered by the book featured masses of wheeling, shooting chariots manned by *maryannu*-style aristocratic nobilities, their rulers defined by the size of their chariot corps.

With the Minoans and Mycenaeans, we return to the spear-armed phalanx to provide the backbone for armies again led by chariot riding aristocracies, showing the high levels of societal organisation evident in Crete and later Greece at the time. The huge levels of economic dislocation around the eastern Mediterranean, caused by the climate change-related catastrophic event around 1,250 BC, is then very visible, given that the Sea Peoples who emerged were nowhere near as sophisticated as warriors, despite their ferocity. Note should also be made here of the maritime prowess of these city-states and peoples.

One eye-opening fact for this author when researching the book was how successful the early Hebrew tribes were in their military activities, following their return to Canaan. They always appear punching well above their weight when tackling far more sophisticated opponents. With the onset of the United and Divided Monarchies, we then see them taking their place amongst the myriad of kingdoms and city-states of the Levant at the end of the 2nd millennium BC and into the 1st millennium BC. By the time of the Israel and Judah, these kingdoms could match the military establishments of all of their opponents, excepting mighty Assyria and Babylon, whom they crossed to their severe detriment and ultimate demise.

This brings us onto the great militaristic titans of *Old Testament Warriors*. These are the mighty Hittite, Assyrian and Babylonian kingdoms and empires through all the phases of their existence. The Hittites proved very resilient, and certainly benefited from the wide variety of cultures, either within their empire or without it, as their vassals and allies. Muwatalli II's victory over the Ramesses II at Kadesh in 1,274 BC marks the highlight of their military prowess. I will next briefly touch on the Babylonians out of sequence, with Nebuchadnezzar II leading them to their greatest glory. However, it is the Assyrians who to my mind deserve the greatest plaudits as the leading military establishment covered in this book. This is especially the case as one moves into the Neo-Assyrian period, when it is clear that the entire Assyrian state was geared to supporting its military ambitions, which were huge. As the leaders of Babylon and Elam found out when they stood up to Ashurbanipal, they did so in the knowledge that failure in war against the brutal Assyrians would come with the severest possible consequences for themselves, their people and their state. The Assyrians were also great military innovators, whether in the context of their huge late-period war chariots, adoption of full cavalry or their sophisticated siege technology that meant few urban centres were safe from their attentions.

Next, I briefly reflect on the importance of literacy in the book. It is clear that among all the cultures covered in *Old Testament Warriors*, the ability to use symbolic script in many forms was one of the key factors allowing the civilisations and cultures mentioned here to thrive. Certainly, for us today, they provide huge insight into the lives of the people detailed from so long ago, creating a direct link from that time to this. This is not just at the top of society, with, for example, the exploits of Sargon the Great or Ashurbanipal, but also at lower levels of society too. This is particularly the case with the military establishments of these peoples given their centrality to the states in the period covered.

This leads us elegantly onto the legacy left to us today from these peoples of these far-off times. While clearly many people in this huge region still identify a lineage with their forebears there, here, the focus is only on the military aspect. We see throughout the book the development of some of the key elements of conflict in the pre-modern world. These include the use of various equid-related mounted troops, usually the elite component of the army, in the form of chariots and later cavalry. The latter were still a battle winning component of armies all the way through to the 19th century AD. In terms of foot troops, many armies covered here were among the first to feature highly organised bodies of warriors. Thus, one can trace a direct lineage from the spear phalanxes of later Sumer and Akkad, through those of the Minoans and Mycenaeans, to the Classical Greek hoplite and Macedonian pikemen, and through the latter to the Renaissance pikemen of the Swiss and Landsknechts. Similarly, naval power is first visible among the nations covered here, and again one can draw a direct line from the monoreme galleys of the Levant through the triremes of Classical Greece and through to the huge galleasses of Renaissance Spain, Genoa and Venice. Finally, the twinned skills of fortification and siege-craft first emerge in our period, which by its end saw all the great cities in all of the regions covered here circled by massive fortifications, and an arms race in full flow as besiegers sought new ways to crack their way in. This was to remain the case all the way through to the advent of gunpowder.

My final personal note is to reflect back to the very beginning of the book and the building of the Pre-Pottery Neolithic A (PPNA) wall circuit in Jericho. I still find this an astonishing example of military engineering, with an individual, or individuals, actually sitting down to design and then build this amazing defensive circuit between 8,250 and 7,600 BC, with no prior experience to guide them given its scale. Over and above the context of warfare as I define it in Chapter 1, this is truly human ingenuity at its best and brightest.

Further Reading

Healy, M. (1991). *The Ancient Assyrians*. Osprey Publishing.

Healy, M. (2000). *Warriors of the Old Testament*. Brockhampton Press.

Keller, W. (2015). *The Bible as History*. William Morrow and Company.

Leick, G. (2002). *Mesopotamia: The Invention of the City*. Penguin.

Stillman, N. and Tallis, N. (1984) *Armies of the Ancient Near East: 3,000 BC to 539 BC*. Wargames Research Group.

The Holy Bible, King James Version.

Van De Mieroop, M. (2015). *A History of the Ancient Near East, Ca 3000 BC-323 BC*. John Wiley and Sons.

Acknowledgements

I would like to thank the many people who have helped make *Old Testament Warriors* possible. Specifically, as always, Professor Andrew Lambert of the War Studies Department at KCL, Dr Andrew Gardner at UCL's Institute of Archaeology and Dr Steve Willis at the University of Kent. All continue to give much appreciated encouragement and guidance with regard to my writing projects. Next, my publisher, Casemate Publishers, and specifically, Ruth Sheppard and Isobel Fulton. Also, Professor Sir Barry Cunliffe of the School of Archaeology at Oxford University, and Professor Martin Millett at the Faculty of Classics, Cambridge University. Next, my patient proof-reader and lovely wife Sara, and my dad John Elliott for being my partner in crime in various escapades researching this book. As with all of my literary work, all have contributed greatly and freely, enabling this work on Old Testament Warriors to reach fruition. Finally, of course, I would like to thank my family, especially my tolerant wife Sara, once again, and children Alex and Lizzie.

Index